Read Me First

- Descriptions in this manual are based on the default settings of Samsung Galaxy S10, S10 Plus and S10e.

- All information supplied in this guide is for ed [barcode] sers bear the responsibility for using it.

- All information supplied in this guide was what was available as at the time of writing this guide and it may not be 100% accurate again if there is a major firmware/software update to Samsung Galaxy S10, S10 Plus or S10e.

- Depending on your local network service provider or your location/region, some of the features discussed in this guide may not be available on your Samsung Galaxy S10, S10 Plus or S10e.

- Some of the fonts contained in the screenshots used in this book have been boldened and enlarged to make it easier to see. You can also bolden or increase the font of your phone by going to **Settings** > **Display** > **Font size and style**. To adjust the font size, drag the slider next to **Font Size**. You would see the preview of the font size at the upper part of the screen. To embolden the font, tap **Bold font**.

- Although I took tremendous effort to ensure that all pieces of information provided in this guide are correct, I would welcome your suggestions if you find out that any information provided in this guide is inadequate, or if you find a better way of doing some of the actions mentioned in this guide. All correspondences should be sent to pharmibrahimguides@gmail.com.

About This Guide

Finally, a simplified guide on Samsung Galaxy S10, S10 Plus and S10e is here – I believe you are going to find this guide a splendid companion for the use of these phones.

A very thorough, no-nonsense guide useful for both experts and newbies, this guide contains a lot of vital information on the use of Samsung Galaxy S10, S10 Plus and S10e.

It is full of actionable steps, hints, notes, screenshots and suggestions. This guide is specifically written for newbies/beginners and seniors; nonetheless, I strongly believe that even the tech-savvy among us will find some benefits reading it.

Enjoy yourself as you go through this very comprehensive guide.

PS: Please make sure you do not give a gift of Samsung Galaxy S10, S10 Plus or S10e without giving this companion guide alongside with it. This guide will make your gift a complete one.

Table of Contents

How to Use This Guide (Please Read!)

This guide is an unofficial manual of Samsung Galaxy S10, S10 Plus or S10e and it should be used just like you use any reference book or manual.

To quickly find a topic, please use the table of contents. In addition, you can use the search menu in your reading app to search for any word or phrase in this guide. This would allow you to quickly find information and save time.

When I say you should carry out a set of tasks, for example, when I say you should tap **Settings > Sound > Notifications & actions**, what I mean is that you should tap on **Settings** and then tap on **Sound**. And lastly, you should tap on **Notifications & actions**. Finally, when a function is enabled or turned on, the status switch will appear boldened and colored. On the other hand, when a function is disabled or turned off, the status switch will appear gray.

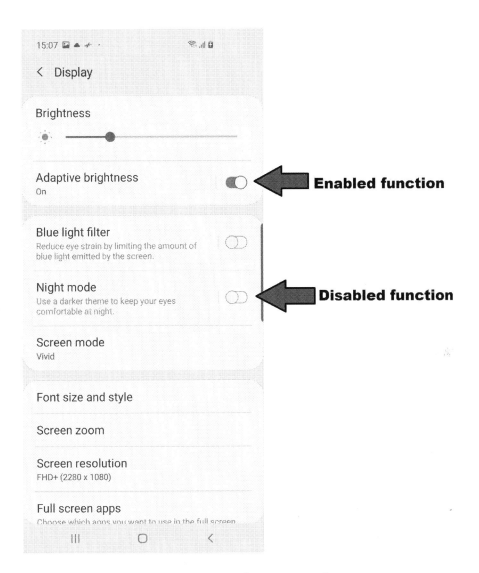

I hope this guide helps you get the most out of your smartphone.

Getting Started with Your Phone

Unpacking Your Device

It is quite easy to unbox your Samsung Galaxy S10, S10 Plus or S10e. Just use your hand to press the inner box until it slides out (if needed). Then use a knife to cut the seal (if any) and carefully open the box.

When you unpack your product box, check your product box for the following items:

1. Samsung Galaxy S10, S10 Plus or S10e
2. USB charging cable & power adapter
3. Quick Start Guide
4. Earphones
5. USB connector (USB Type-C)
6. Eject Pin (the eject pin is located on the case that house the "quick start guide")
7. Micro USB Connector.

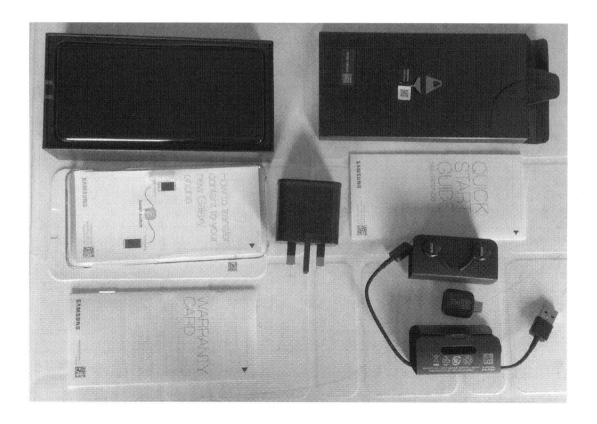

Tip: I would advise that you are careful while removing the eject pin from the case (the eject pin is located on the case that houses the "quick start guide") so as not to prick your hand in the process.

Turning Your Phone On/Off and Setting Up Your Phone

Just like many other smartphones, turning on your device is as simple as ABC. To turn on your phone, press and hold the power key (see the picture below) until you sense a little vibration. If you are turning on your phone for the first time, please carefully follow the on-screen instructions to set it up. You will have the option to connect to a Wireless network during the setup, to learn more about connecting your phone to Wi-Fi, please go to page 353. In addition, I would recommend that you insert the SIM Card before switching on your phone. To learn more about inserting the SIM card, see page 25.

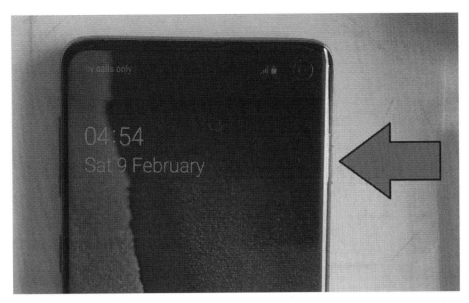

To turn off your phone, press and hold the power key and select **Power off.** Select **Power off** again to confirm.

Tip: If you don't feel like switching off your phone again and you want to dismiss the power off screen, simply tap the back button. Alternatively, tap anywhere outside the onscreen icons.

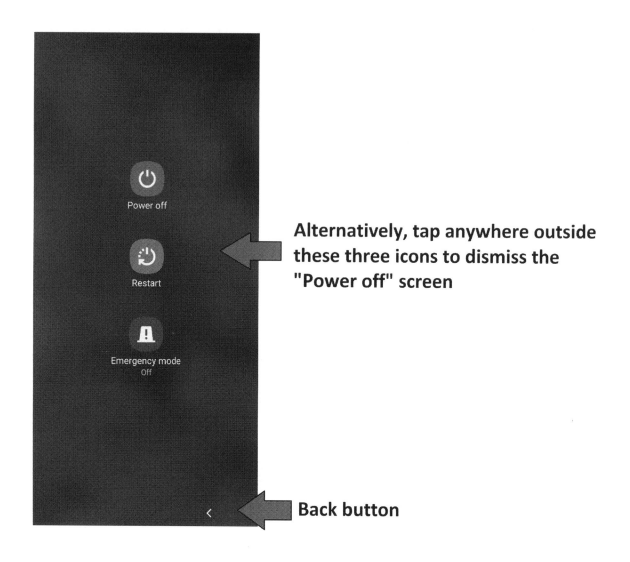

Alternatively, tap anywhere outside these three icons to dismiss the "Power off" screen

Back button

In addition, if you are using the phone for the first time, remove any protective film from the surface of the phone.

Please do not be annoyed if you find it unnecessary learning about how to on/off your device. I have included it in case there may be someone reading this guide who is a complete novice and knows close to nothing about smartphones.

Tips:

- Some network providers may require you to enter a PIN when you switch on your phone. You can try entering **0000** or **1234**. This is the default PIN for many network providers. If you have a problem entering the correct PIN, please contact your network service provider.

- During the setup, you may skip a process by tapping **Skip** (usually) located at the bottom of the screen. Usually, you will have the option to perform this process in the future by going to the phone settings.

- While using your phone for the first time, you may have the option to transfer your contents from your old phone to your new Samsung device. Just carefully follow the on-screen instructions to do this. If you skip the process of content transfer during the phone setup and you will like to perform the transfer now, please see page 41 to 45 to learn how to go about this.

- Because of software updates and installations, it is likely that your new Samsung Galaxy device will consume a large amount of data during the setup, I would recommend that you connect to a wireless network if you can. Using a mobile network during the setup might be expensive.

- When you start using Samsung Galaxy S10, S10 Plus or S10e, you may probably notice that its screen locks within a few seconds after you finish interacting with it. To allow the screen to stay longer before it locks, change the screen timeout setting. To do this:

  - Swipe down from the top of the screen and select settings icon .
  - Tap **Display**.
  - Scroll down and tap on **Screen Timeout**. Then choose an option.

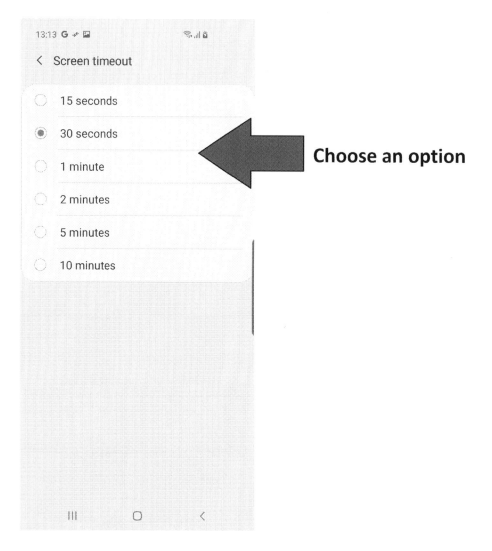

Please note that selecting a longer timeout may make your battery discharge faster.

Do you need to charge your phone before first use?

Samsung recommends that your charge your Samsung S10, S10 Plus or S10e before the first use. I would recommend you do this whenever you can.

However, if there is no way to charge it, then you can use it straightaway without charging it. I have learnt that it is not compulsory you charge the new lithium batteries now used in recent smartphones before first use (provided that the battery still has power).

Get to Know Your Device

Device Layout

Please note that Samsung Galaxy S10, Samsung Galaxy S10 Plus and Samsung Galaxy S10e look very similar except for few differences. In the picture shown below, I have used Samsung Galaxy S10 as an example.

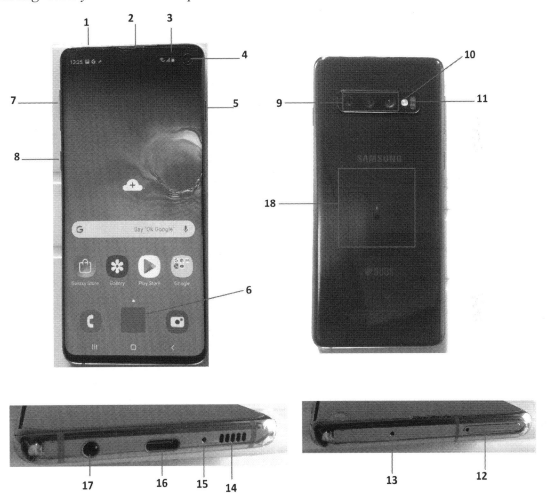

Number	Function
1.	SIM and memory card tray
2.	Speaker
3.	Proximity/light sensors. The GPS antenna is also located around this area
4.	Front camera. Unlike Galaxy S10/S10e, Galaxy S10+ has two front cameras
5.	Power button
6.	Approximate location of the fingerprint sensor. The fingerprint sensor of Galaxy S10e is found on the power button.
7.	Volume button
8.	Bixby button
9.	Back cameras. Galaxy S10e has dual cameras while Galaxy S10 and S10+ has triple cameras
10.	Flash light
11.	Heart rate sensor. Samsung Galaxy S10e does not have Heart rate sensor. Instead, the Light sensor of S10e is found where Heart rate sensor is supposed to be.
12.	SIM and memory card tray
13.	Microphone
14.	Speaker
15.	Microphone
16.	USB port and charging port (multipurpose port)
17.	Headset jack
18.	NFC (Near Field Communication) antenna/MST (Magnetic Secure Transmission) antenna/Wireless charging coil

Tip: You can measure your heart rate with your Samsung Galaxy S10 or S10 Plus. To do this, from the application screen, tap on **Samsung Health** app. Then carefully follow the onscreen instructions to setup the app (if you have not done so before). Thereafter, scroll down and tap on **Measure** next to **Heart rate**.

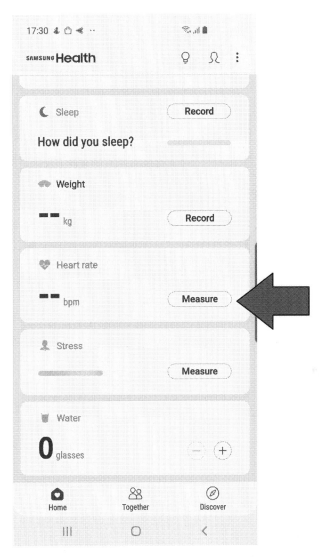

Tap **Allow** when prompted (if you agree). Then place your finger on the heart rate sensor (found next to the flash light) and allow your phone to measure your heart rate. Please note that Samsung Galaxy S10e does not have heart rate sensor.

Swiping the Screen Properly

From time to time, you would need to interact with your phone by swiping the screen with your finger. If you don't swipe it properly, you may not get the desired result. You can swipe to perform the following actions:

1. **Access the notification menu or quick settings**

To access the notification menu or quick settings, swipe down from the top of the screen. Please make sure you are starting from the top of the screen (around the earpiece/receiver area) to get the desired result. See the picture below.

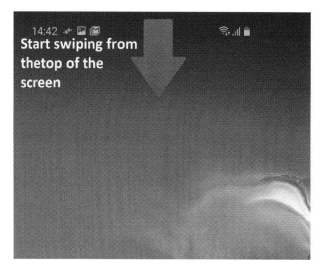

If you don't start swiping from the top of the screen, you might open the applications screen instead.

2. **Accessing the app screen**

To access the applications screen, swipe up from the lower part of the screen. See the direction of the arrow below.

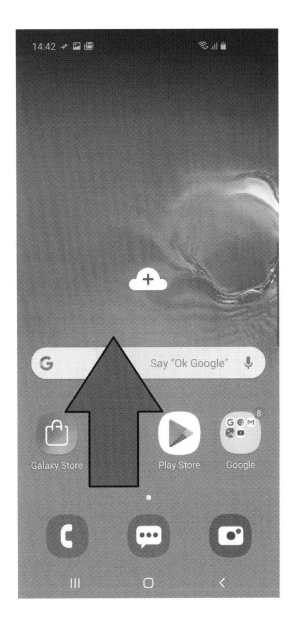

To go back to the home screen while on the applications screen, just swipe up or down from the middle (or around the middle) of the screen.

Get to Know the Settings Tab

I think it is cool I introduce you to the settings tab because I would be referring to this tab a lot.

The settings tab has many subsections and because of this, I would advise you use the **Search** menu (denoted by the lens icon Q) to quickly find what you are looking for. To use the settings search feature, swipe down from the top of the screen and tap the settings icon (see the picture below).

Then tap on the search icon Q and type a keyword corresponding to the settings you are looking for. For example, if you are looking for settings relating to battery, just type **Battery** into the search bar. The result filters as you type.

Tip: You can search the settings with your voice instead of typing. To use this feature, just tap the microphone button 🎤 and say a word or a phrase. For example, you may say **battery** if you want to search for settings relating to battery.

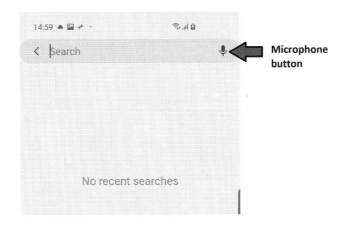

To search another phrase or word, simply tap the **X** icon next to the present word/phrase, tap the microphone button 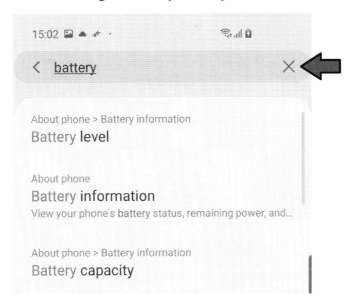 again and say a new phrase/word.

Hint: You might want to change the name of your Samsung Galaxy to your name. To do this, go to **Settings** > **About Phone** (the last item in the list). Then click on **Edit** (under the phone's name) and enter a new name. Other phones should see the new name when they want to connect via Bluetooth.

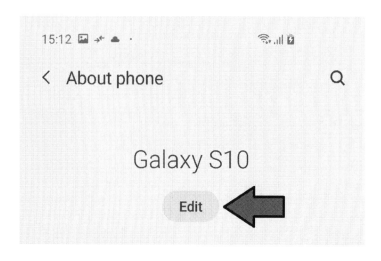

Charging Your Device

If you use your Samsung Galaxy S10, S10 Plus or S10e more often (especially if you use Wi-Fi frequently), you may realize that you need to charge your phone every day or twice a day. One of the coolest times to charge your device is when you are taking a shower, as you are not likely to be using it at the time.

Do you need to charge your phone before the first use?

Please see the answer on page 6.

Tip: To learn more on how to use your phone for a longer time on battery, please go to page 375.

To charge your Samsung Galaxy S10, S10 Plus or S10e:

1. When you first open your product box, you will notice that the power cord consists of two parts (i.e. the USB cable and the USB power adapter), connect these two parts together. See the picture below.

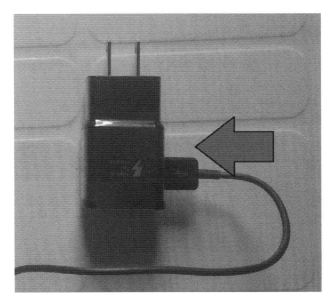

2. Connect the end of the USB cable to the charging port of your device, making sure that both the charging cable and the charging port on your device make a good and firm contact.

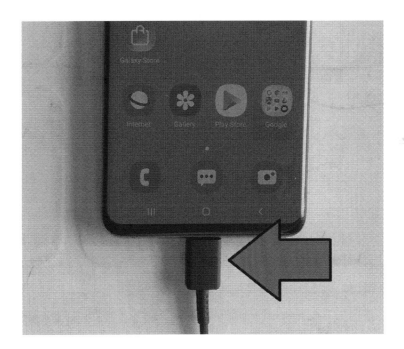

3. Plug the power adapter to an electrical outlet. When your phone is charging, a charging icon 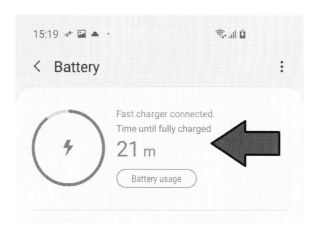 will appear at the top of the screen. When your phone is fully charged, the battery icon will appear solid/full.

Tip: After charging, you may need to apply a small force to remove the USB cord from the phone. Please be careful so that the phone does not mistakenly drop from your hand in the process.

4. To know the estimated charging time remaining, swipe down from the top of the screen and tap **Settings** ⚙ > **Device care** > **Battery**. The charging time may be longer if you are using your device while charging it.

Tips:

- To know the detailed usage of your battery since your phone was last fully charged, go to **Settings** ⚙ > **Device care** > **Battery** > **Battery Usage**.

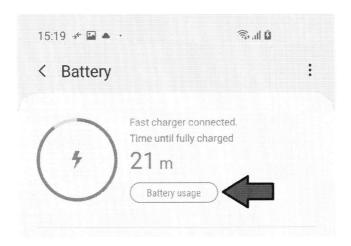

- To have the battery percentage shown at the top of the screen, do the following: Swipe down from the top of the screen using two fingers and select the menu icon ⋮ . Then select **Status bar** and tap the status switch next to **Show battery percentage**.

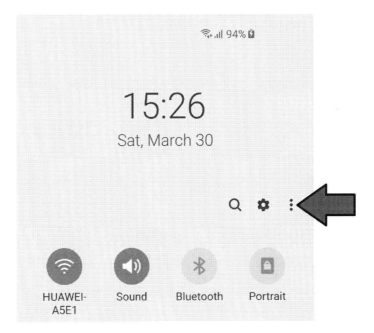

- To extend the power of your device substantially, swipe down from the top of the screen and tap **Settings** ⚙ > **Device care** > **Battery** > **Power Mode**. Then select an option.

*To allow your phone to adjust its power features based on your usage of the phone, select **Adaptive power saving**.*

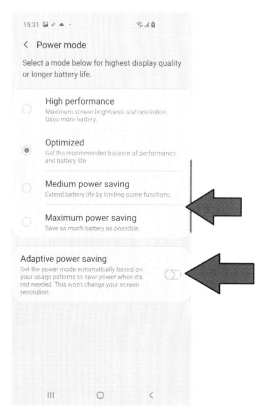

Troubleshooting Tip: Please note that if you choose **Medium power saving** or **Maximum power saving**, your phone may cause some app or functions to stop working properly in order to save battery. If you see that some apps or features are not working as they should, check if you have not enabled Medium or Maximum power saving mode.

- There are some apps out there that will consume your battery even without using them. Interestingly, you can prevent these apps from doing this. To do this, swipe down from the top of the screen and tap settings ⚙ > **Device care** > **Battery**. Under **Usage by apps** tab, select an app you want to restrict, and tap **Put app to sleep**. Please note that you may not be able to put all apps to sleep.

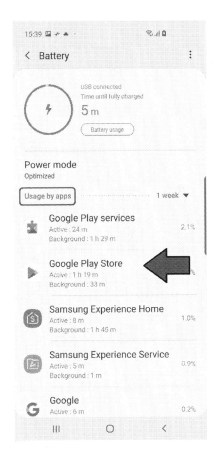

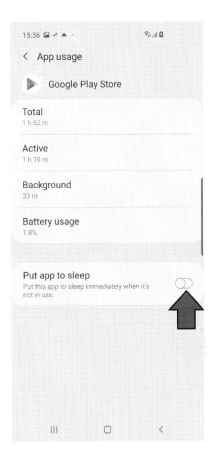

- Alternatively, if you do not want an app to consume your battery by running in the background, you can put it to sleep by doing the following:

a. Swipe down from the top of the screen and tap settings  > **Device care** > **Battery.**

b. Then select the menu icon ⋮ found at the top of the screen and select **Settings**.

c. Select **Sleeping apps** and then tap **Add**. Select the apps you want and tap **Add**.

To remove an app from **Sleeping apps** tab, repeat steps **a** and **b** above. Select **Sleeping apps**. Then tap and hold the app(s) you want to remove. Tap **Remove** (located at the bottom of the screen).

Warning: Please note that it is not advisable to use the multipurpose port while it is wet. If your phone has contact with water or any watery substance, please make sure you dry the multipurpose port before using it. Although Samsung Galaxy S10, S10 Plus and S10e are water resistant, it is not advisable at all to charge it while the device is wet. This may cause an electric shock or damage your device.

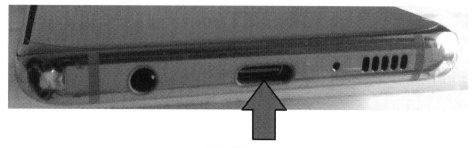

Multipurpose jack

Using the Fast Charging Feature

Your device is built with a battery charging technology that charges the battery faster by increasing the charging power. This feature can allow you to charge the device up to 50% in about 40-45 minutes. Interestingly, Samsung Galaxy S10, S10 Plus and S10e supports fast cable charging and fast wireless charging.

Please note that using your phone while charging may affect the time your phone is going to take to make a complete charging cycle.

Tip: You can enable or disable the fast charging settings by going to Settings >

Device care > **Battery**. Then tap on menu icon located at the top of the screen. Select **Settings** > **Fast cable charging**.

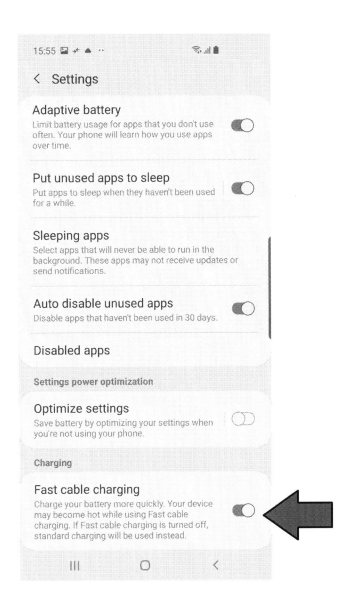

Furthermore, you might not be able to use the fast charging feature when you charge the battery using a standard battery/phone charger. To use **Fast Charging** on your device, you might need to connect it to a battery charger that supports Adaptive fast charging like the one that came with your device. To know if a battery charger supports this feature, check the charger for an *Adaptive fast charging* inscription.

Although, the fast charging technology on Samsung Galaxy S10, S10 Plus and S10e is a cool feature, it may still be affected by factors like the temperature of the phone. If the device heats up for one reason or the other, the charging speed may decrease.

What About the Wireless Charging?

Samsung Galaxy S10, S10 Plus and S10e has a built-in wireless charging feature and this means that you can charge your device's battery using a wireless charger (sold separately).

To charge your device wirelessly:

- Connect the power adapter that came with your wireless charger (sold separately) to the charging port on your wireless charger. Thereafter, plug it (power adapter) to a wall socket.

- If you are using your wireless charger for the first time, remove any protective film from the surface of the wireless charger. Then, place your mobile device on the wireless charger following the instructions provided by the manufacturer of the wireless charger. Please note that if you connect a charger to your mobile device during wireless charging, the wireless charging feature might be unavailable. *I will also recommend you avoid doing so.*

In addition, depending on the type of the wireless charger you are using, charging wirelessly may take a longer time when compared to using a cable. This means that if you want to charge your device faster, consider using a cable.

Protection Tip: To avoid damaging your phone or heating up your phone, please ensure there is no foreign object between the wireless charger and your phone. Foreign objects include (but not limited to) metals, credit cards and magnets.

The Wireless PowerShare

One of the things that make Samsung Galaxy S10, S10 Plus and S10e stand out is the ability to charge other devices that support wireless charging. If you have much power on your phone, you could easily share it with family and friends by placing a device on the back of the phone. You may need to enable this option as it may not be enabled by default. To do this:

1. Swipe down from the top of the screen using two fingers.
2. Tap on Wireless PowerShare button to activate it. You may need to double-tap it to activate it. When the Wireless PowerShare is enabled, its icon would appear boldened.

Notes:

- If the battery of your phone drops below a certain amount, you might be unable to use the PowerShare feature.
- If you charge your device while using the PowerShare, the charging speed might reduce.
- It is recommended not to use earphones while using the PowerShare.

Inserting and Managing SD Card or SIM Card

Samsung Galaxy S10, S10 Plus and S10e supports the use of external memory card.

To insert memory card or SIM card:

1. Locate the SIM and SD card tray on the top edge of the device and gently insert the eject tool included with your phone into the eject hole (located at the top edge of your phone). Then push until the tray pops out (see the picture below). *Please note that you may need to apply a small force before the tray pops out.*

2. Pull out the tray gently from the tray slot and place the SIM card on its tray and the SD Card on its tray. Make sure the metallic contacts on the SIM and the SD card are facing down.

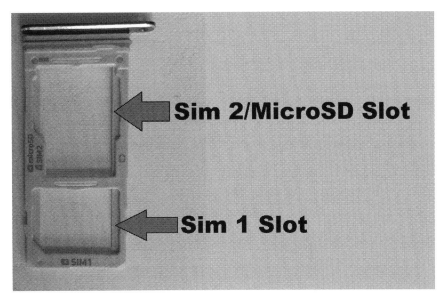

Tip: *Please note that SIM 2 would not be available on your phone if you don't buy the dual SIM version. In addition, if you are using the dual SIM version, you may not be able to use a second SIM and the external memory card at the same time. This is because both the second SIM (SIM 2) and the external memory card use the same space.*

*However, you may still be able to get a second SIM and external memory card to work simultaneously if you use a dual SIM adapter. Just search for **dual SIM adapter** on amazon.com to get started.*

After inserting the SIM and memory card, the whole setup will look like this. See the picture below.

3. Slide the card tray back into the slot.

4. Please note that if the SIM card or the memory card is not inserted properly, your phone might not recognize it. Please endeavor to follow the instructions provided above to avoid this.

5. To locate the memory card after inserting it, swipe up from the bottom of the screen and tap **Samsung** folder > **My Files**. Then tap the **SD Card** folder.

Note: Since Samsung Galaxy S10, S10 Plus or S10e device is water resistant, you may be tempted to drop it in water at one time or the other. Please make sure that you fully insert the card tray into the tray slot before dropping the phone inside water so as to prevent liquid from entering your device.

As a rule, you must always make sure you prevent water from entering the inner compartment of the phone. Therefore, please make sure you properly close any slot you have opened on your phone before dipping it into water. Also make sure the memory card tray is not wet when you want to insert it back into the memory card slot.

Tip: To access the memory card go to **Settings** > **Device care** > **Storage** > **SD card**.

To remove the SD Card:

1. Swipe down from the top of the screen and select the settings icon .
2. Scroll down and tap **Device care**.

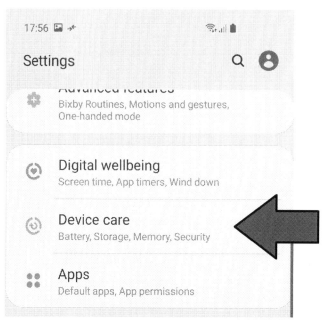

3. Tap **Storage**.

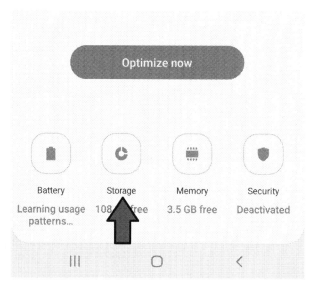

4. Tap the **menu icon** (the three dots icon located at the top of the screen).

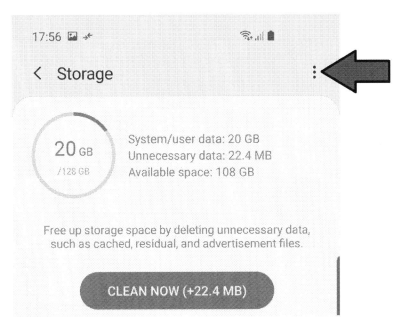

5. Tap **Storage settings**.

6. Tap the unmount icon ▲ and gently open the SD card slot using the ejection pin (as you have done above). Close the SD card slot when you are done removing the memory card.

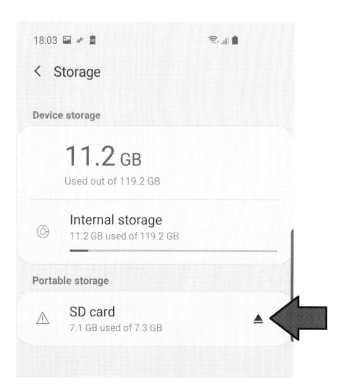

Please note that if you unmount the memory card without removing it from your device, you would need to mount it before it can be accessed again. To mount your memory card, follow the steps one to five above and tap **Unmounted**. Then select **Mount** when prompted.

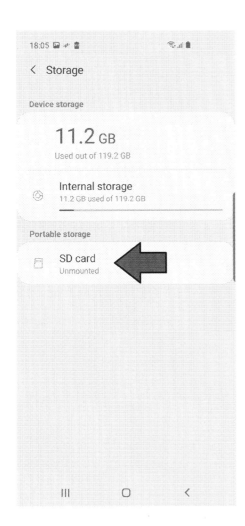 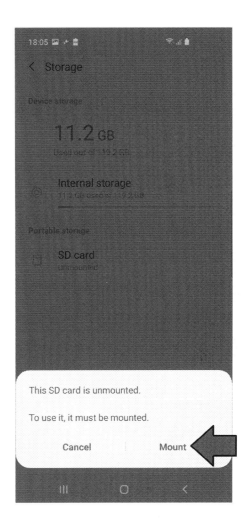

Encrypt SD Card

You may wish to encrypt your memory card for extra security.

- From the Home screen, swipe up from the bottom of the screen and tap **Settings.**

- Tap **Biometrics and security**

- Scroll down and tap **Encrypt SD card**.

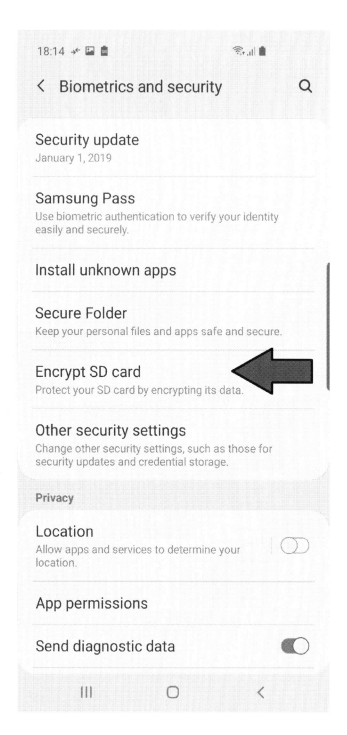

- Please read all the on-screen information that appears.

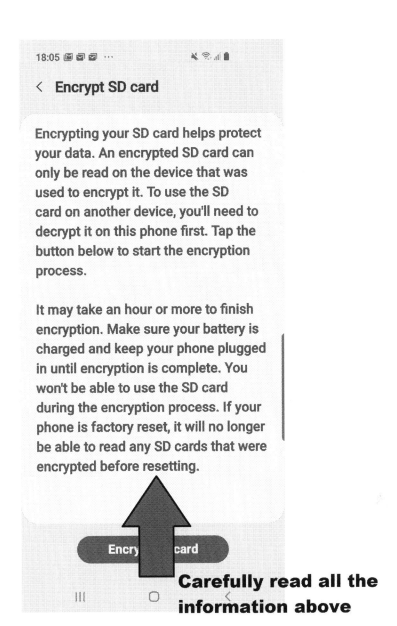

18:05

< Encrypt SD card

Encrypting your SD card helps protect your data. An encrypted SD card can only be read on the device that was used to encrypt it. To use the SD card on another device, you'll need to decrypt it on this phone first. Tap the button below to start the encryption process.

It may take an hour or more to finish encryption. Make sure your battery is charged and keep your phone plugged in until encryption is complete. You won't be able to use the SD card during the encryption process. If your phone is factory reset, it will no longer be able to read any SD cards that were encrypted before resetting.

Encry   card

Carefully read all the information above

- If you are satisfied with the information, tap **Encrypt SD card** located at the bottom of the screen and follow the on-screen instructions to encrypt all the data on your memory card.

When you encrypt your memory card, you may need a numeric PIN or password to decrypt your SD card when you first access it after switching on your device. In addition, *please note that encrypting a memory card may make it unreadable on another device. In addition, please note that if you reset your device to factory default settings, it will be unable to read the SD card you have encrypted. It is therefore recommended you decrypt it on your phone first before resetting your phone.*

Formatting the memory card

1. Swipe down from the top of the screen and select the settings icon .
2. Tap **Device care**.
3. Tap **Storage.**
4. Tap the **menu icon** (the three dots icon located at the top of the screen)**.**

5. Then select **Storage settings**
6. Tap **SD card**. (Please make sure you tap the "SD card" and not the unmount icon next to it).

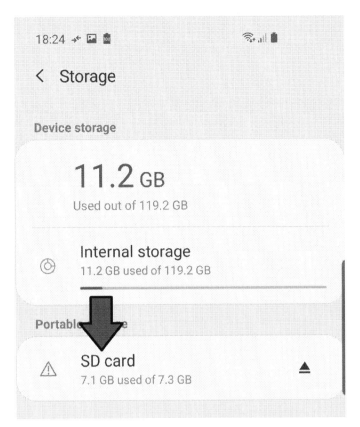

7. Tap **Format**, read the on-screen information and tap **Format SD card**.

Please note that formatting a memory card will cause you to lose all the files stored on the memory card. You may need to backup your files before initiating this process.

To transfer apps from internal storage to SD Card:
Please note that many apps don't allow you to move them to the SD card.

1. Swipe down from the top of the screen and tap **Settings** .
2. Tap **Apps**.
3. Tap the app you want to transfer.
4. Select **Storage** from the options that appear.
5. Under the name of the app you want to transfer, tap **Change**.

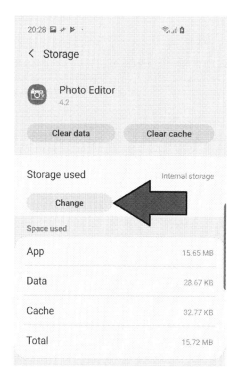

6. Tap **SD card.**
7. Tap **Move** located at bottom of the screen and wait for the process to finish.

Tip: You may consider removing temporary files from your device to free up space. From the Home screen, swipe up from the bottom of the screen and tap **Settings** > **Device care**. Tap **Storage** and tap **Clean Now**.

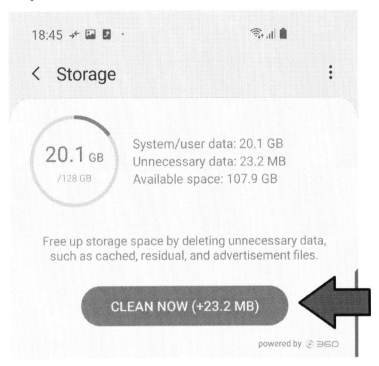

Please note that using this method may clear cached data for all apps. Cache data can loosely be defined as temporary files from an application or website stored on your device to ease your interaction with the application or website.

Tip: If your phone is hanging or misbehaving, consider cleaning the memory. To do this, from the Home screen, swipe up from the bottom of the screen and tap **Settings > Device care**. Tap **Memory** and tap **Clean Now.**

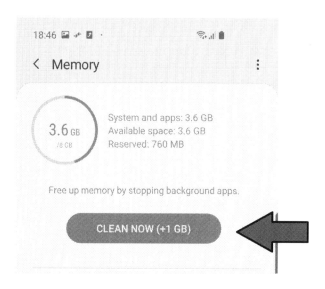

Maintaining the Water and Dust Resistance

Although your Samsung Galaxy S10, S10 Plus and S10e are water and dust resistant, there are a few things you still have to put at the back of your mind so that you don't damage your phone. Some of the things you have to know are discussed below:

- Even though your device is water resistant, you can't still immerse the device in water deeper than 1.5 m and/or keep it submerged for more than 30 minutes.

- The water you want to put your phone inside should be fresh water and it should have a temperature range between 15 - 35°C and pressure range between 86 and 106 kPa.

- The screen of your device may not respond properly while under water or wet. I will advice that you clean it with a dry towel to get back the full functionality.

- It is not advisable to put your device under water moving with force such as tap water. This is because water may get into the inner part of your device in the process.

- While the phone's screen is wet, you may not enjoy the optimal function of your device as you should. You may need to clean it with a dry towel to make it work properly.

- To avoid electric shock or damage to your phone, please don't charge your device while it is wet or under water.
- If your phone falls from a considerable height, it may affect its water resistivity.
- Never put your phone under water while the SIM/SD card tray is out.
- Avoid putting your phone in a liquid other than water. In addition, avoid putting your phone inside salt water or ionized water.

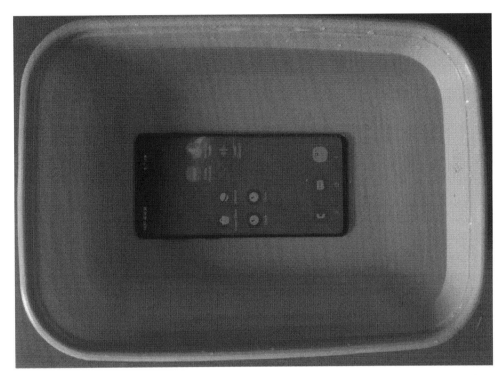

Tip: Samsung Galaxy S10, S10 Plus or S10e may not respond to touch while under water but it should respond to touch after you take it out of water. But don't forget that you shouldn't drop it in water while the SIM/memory slot is opened. In addition, please don't charge your phone while it is wet to avoid electric shock or damage to your phone.

Moving Your Items from Your Old Phone to Your device

You can move your files to your new phone by following the steps mentioned below:

- One of the easiest ways to transfer your items from your old phone (Android Phone or IOS Phone) to your new Samsung Galaxy S10, S10 Plus or S10e is by using a USB connector (On-the-Go (OTG) connector) and a USB cable. To use this method, please follow the instructions below:

Please make sure you download and install Smart Switch app on your old phone before you begin the transfer process. Smart Switch can be downloaded from Google Play Store. In addition, this method of data transfer consumes a considerable amount of energy, make sure your phone is fully charged before initiating this process.

To transfer content via cable:

- Plug the USB connector (On-the-Go (OTG) connector) that came with your device into the multipurpose jack of your device.

- Then connect your device and the old phone using a USB cable. Please note that you are to select Media device (MTP) option on your old phone if prompted. The whole connection would look like the picture below. *Please note that you may need to download, install and open Samsung Smart Switch Mobile on your old phone to complete this process.* **Samsung Smart Switch Mobile** app can be downloaded from Google Play Store.

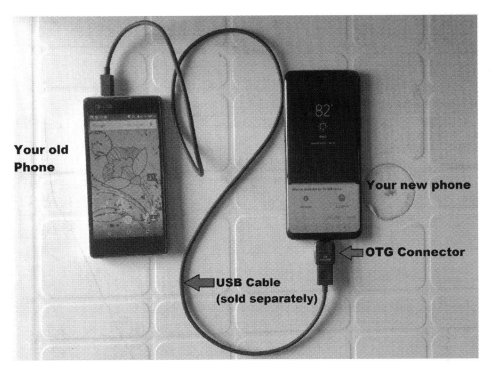

- When prompted, tap **Smart Switch** and select **Just Once**. If you are not prompted, disconnect the cable, then reconnect.

- Tap **Agree** if you agree with the terms/condition.

- Read the onscreen instructions and select **Start**.

- On the old phone open **Samsung Smart Switch Mobile** app and follow the prompts.

- Tap **Receive data** on your Samsung Galaxy S10, S10 Plus or S10e.

- Your device will recognize the old phone and a list of data you can transfer will appear. Tap to select or deselect items that appear. After selecting what you want to send, select **Transfer/Send** to commence the file transfer.

- Follow the on-screen instructions to complete the data transfer process.

- Alternatively, if the USB connector and the USB cable are not accessible, you can send items from your old phone to your new phone wirelessly using the Smart Switch app. Please note that you will need to download and install **Samsung Smart Switch Mobile** app on your old phone to complete this process. In addition, you would need to switch on the Wi-Fi on your new and old phone to use this option.

To transfer content wirelessly:

- On your device, swipe up from the bottom of the screen to access app screen. Tap **Settings** and select the search icon $\mathcal{Q}$. Enter **Smart Switch** into the search bar and select **Smart Switch** (the first item in the list) from the search results. Then select **Smart Switch** again. Thereafter, tap **Agree > Start > Receive Data > Wireless**. Then select your old phone type.

- Open the **Smart Switch** app on your old phone.

- Tap **Agree** and tap **Start**. Then tap **Send Data**.

- Tap **Wireless.** Thereafter, the Smart Switch app should try to establish connection. If prompted, tap **Accept.**

- On your old phone, select those items you want to transfer and tap **Send**.

- Follow the on-screen instructions on both your device and the old phone to complete the transfer process.

- I would like to mention that you can also transfer items from your old phone to your new device using a memory card. All you have to do is to insert a memory card into your old phone, transfer your content to the memory card, remove the memory card and place it inside your Samsung Galaxy S10, S10 Plus or S10e.

- You could also transfer files from your old phone to your new phone using Wi-Fi Direct (if your old phone has this feature). To use this method of file transfer, enable **Wi-Fi Direct** on your new phone first (you could locate Wi-Fi Direct settings on your new phone by searching for it under the settings tab).

Then select the files you want to transfer on your old phone and tap the share icon $\lessdot$. Select **Wi-Fi Direct**. Your new Samsung phone should automatically display the name of your old phone on its screen. Select this name. On your old/new phone, select **Accept** if prompted.

- Lastly, you can transfer your items from your old phone to your new phone by using cloud storage. For example, you can use OneDrive App. To do this, add files to OneDrive app on your old phone so that you can access them from your new Samsung device. To move a file to OneDrive, simply upload it using the plus Add icon (+) located in the OneDrive app or send the files to your OneDrive folder. Once the files are on OneDrive, you can access them on your Samsung Galaxy S10, S10 Plus or S10e by opening the OneDrive app. To avoid any problem while trying to access your files, please ensure that you are connected to an internet network while trying to access OneDrive.

   Please note that you may need to download OneDrive app to your phones to use this method.

Using the Touch Screen

Your phone's touch screen allows you to easily select items and perform functions.

Notes:

- Do not press the touch screen with sharp tools. Doing so may cause malfunctioning.
- Do not allow the touch screen to come into contact with other electrical appliances. This may cause the touch screen to malfunction.
- When the touch screen is wet, endeavor to clean it with a dry towel before using it. The touchscreen may not function properly when wet.
- For optimal use of the screen, you may need to remove the screen protector before using it. However, a good screen protector should be usable with your phone.

You may control your touch screen with the following actions:

Tap: Touch once with your finger to select or launch a menu, application or option.

Tap and hold: Tap an item and hold it for a second to open a list of options.

Tap and drag: Tap and drag with your finger, to move an item to a different location in the application grid/list.

Pinch: Place two fingers far apart, then draw them closer.

Tip: If you are using a screen protector, you may consider increasing the touch sensitivity of your phone for optimum usage. To do this, swipe up from the bottom of the screen and tap **Settings** 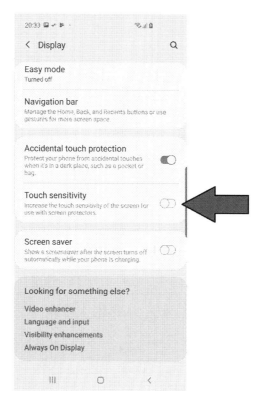 > **Display** > **Touch sensitivity.** Then tap the indicator switch next to **Touch sensitivity**.

Tip: You can control the touch screen with just one hand when you enable one-handed mode. To enable this mode:

1. Swipe down from the top of the screen and tap settings icon .

2. Tap **Advanced features**.

3. Select **Motion and gestures**.

4. Tap **One-handed Mode**.

5. Make sure the status switch is turned **On**. Then select **Button**. When you select **Button**, you would be able to activate one-hand mode by tapping the Home button three times.

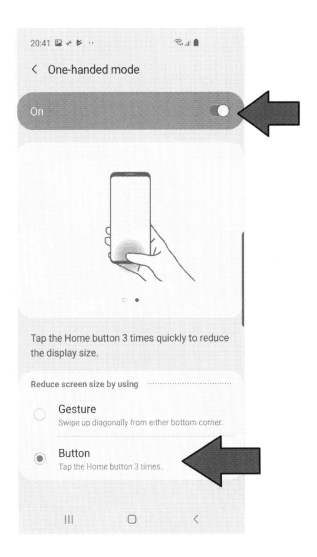

Tip: If you realized that your phone accidentally detects touches when you don't want, for example when the phone is inside your pocket, you could block accidental touches. To do this, go to **Settings** > **Display** > **Accidental touch protection**.

To Lock or Unlock the touch screen

When you do not use the device for a specified period, your device turns off the touch screen and automatically locks so as to prevent any unwanted device operations and save battery. To manually lock the touch screen, press the power key once.

To unlock, turn on the screen by pressing the power key (or double tap the home button

) and swipe up in any direction. If you have already set a lock screen, you will be prompted to enter the lock screen details instead of swiping.

Note: You can change the lock screen type on your phone, please refer to page 124 to learn how to do this.

Rotating the touch screen

Your phone has a built-in motion sensor that detects its orientation. If you rotate the device, the screen should automatically rotate according to the orientation.

➢ **To activate or deactivate screen rotation:**

To quickly disable or enable screen rotation, swipe down from the top of the screen and

tap . Please note that when the screen rotation icon appears gray, the screen rotation is disabled.

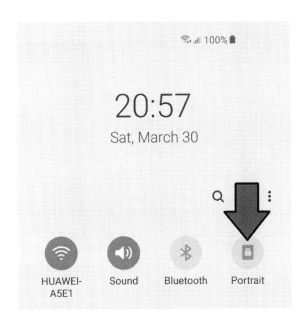

Using the Dedicated Back Button

You may use the dedicated back button (see the picture below) to view the previous page or go back to a previous menu. Back button can also be used to close a dialog box, menu, or keyboard.

In addition, you may use the dedicated back button on your device to get out of any page when you are done with the page and you don't see the "done" option.

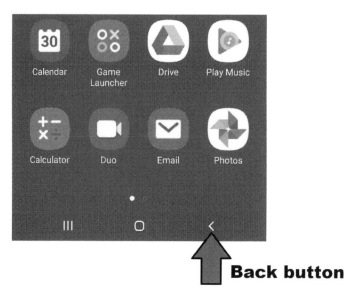

Back button

Tip: Back button is one of the components of the navigation bar. To learn how to manage the navigation bar like a pro, please go to page 92.

Using the In-APP Back Button

There are some apps that give you the opportunity to go back to the previous screen using

the in-app back button ⟨ . When available, this button can be found at the upper left part of the screen.

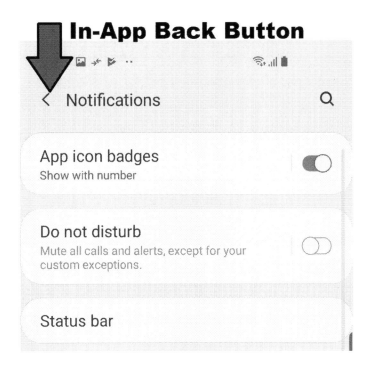

Getting to Know the Menu icon

The menu icon is the three dots icon that usually appears at the top of the screen when you open an app. This icon can also be called **hidden options icon**. This is because it contains more options about an app or item.

Tip: Whenever you are thinking of accessing more options when using an app/item or you are thinking of using an app in a new way, just tap on the menu icon.

Getting to Know the Home Screen

From your Home screen, you can view your phone's status and access applications. Scroll left or right to see different apps on the Home screen. Please note that the Home screen usually has many screens and you can add more screens by tapping on +. More on this shortly.

Home Screen Layout

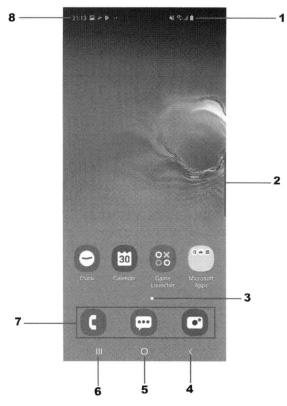

Number	Function
1.	**Status icons**: These icons tell you more about your device. For example, if the Wi-Fi is turned on, you would see the Wi-Fi status icon on the top right part of the screen.
2.	**Edge Handle**: Swipe left on this handle to display edge icons. Go to page 149 to learn more about edge screen.

3.	**Home Screen Indicator:** This indicates which home screen is currently visible
4.	**Back Button**.
5.	**Home Button**
6.	**Recent App button**
7.	**App shortcuts**: Tap any of these icons to launch the corresponding app.
8.	**Notification icon**: When you see a notification icon appearing at the top left part of the screen, simply swipe down from the top of the screen to learn more about this notification icon or see the notification detail.

Customizing the Home Screen

To get more out of the Home screen, you would need to perform some tweaks. To customize the Home screen to your taste:

1. While on the Home screen, place your two fingers on the screen and move them closer or tap and hold an empty space on the Home screen. To go back to the

   Home screen from any point, press the Home button .

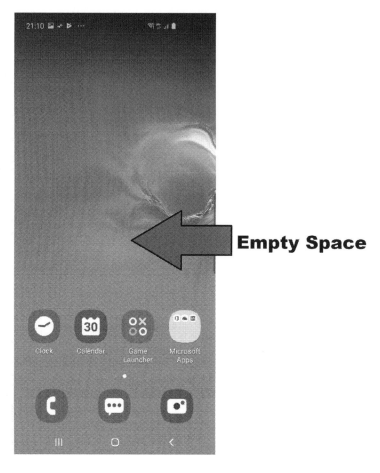

Empty Space

2. Then you will see a screen that looks like the one below.

3. You can perform any of the following actions:

   a) Add a screen: To do this, swipe left until you see the plus/Add **(+)** icon. Tap this icon to add a new screen.

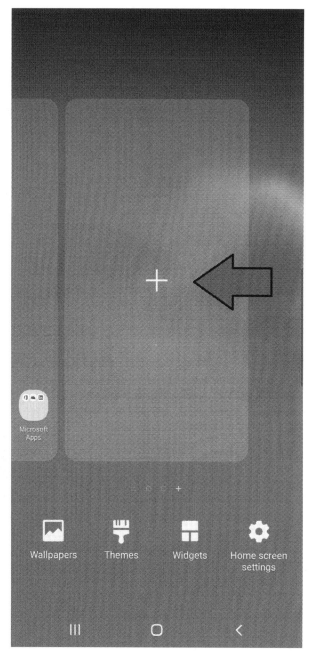

In addition, you can add app icons to a Home screen. To do this, tap and hold an app icon on the applications screen, then select **Add to Home**.

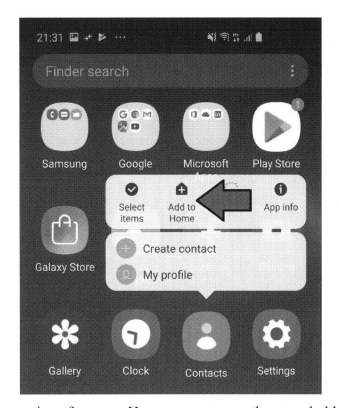

To move an app icon from one Home screen to another, tap, hold and drag the app icon to the edge of the screen and wait for the screen to turn. Do this until you get to the desired screen, then lift your finger.

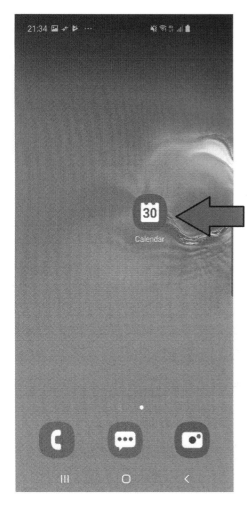

Tap and hold the app icon you want to move, then move it to the right edge or left edge of the screen until the page turns. When the app icon is in the right position, lift your finger.

To move an app icon to another part of a screen, simply tap, hold and drag the icon to the desired part of the screen.

b) Remove a screen: To do this, swipe left until you see the Home screen you want to remove. Then tap the **Delete** icon 🗑 located on top of the screen that you want to delete.

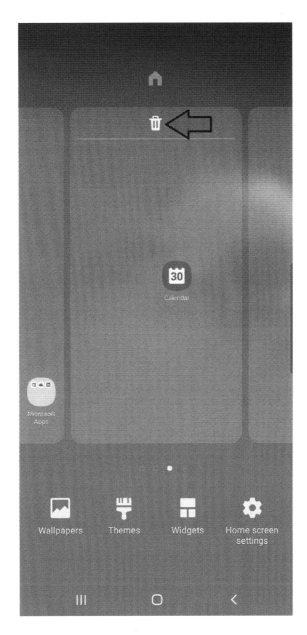

c) Change the order of the Home screens: To do this, tap and hold a screen and drag it to the edge of the screen until the page turns. When the Home screen is in the desired position, lift your finger.

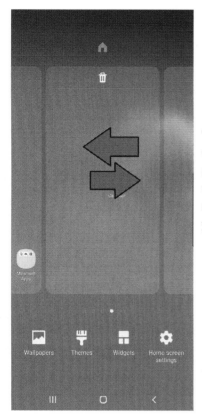

Tap and hold the Home screen you want to move, then move it to the right edge or left edge of the screen until the page turns. When the Home screen is in the right position, lift your finger.

To easily access a Home screen, you may consider setting it as your **main** Home screen. Please see below.

c) Set a screen as the main Home screen: To do this, swipe left or right until the desired screen is visible, then tap the **Home button** located at the top of the screen. When a screen is your main Home screen, the Home screen button appears bold.

Tip: To access the Home screen at any point in time, press the Home button ⬜.

d) Bixby Home: To access Bixby Home, swipe right. To enable or disable this feature, tap the status switch found next to **Bixby Home**. To learn more about Bixby, go to page 168.

Tip: To move out of a setting when you are done, tap the back button.

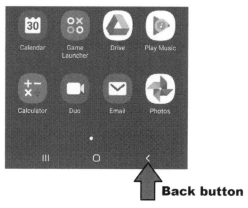

Back button

Hint: Do you want to increase or decrease the number of apps that appear in a row on the Home screen? If yes, go to page 73 to learn more.

Add/Remove an app shortcut to the Home screen

You can add apps/items to the Home screen so that you can easily access them anytime.

To do this:

1. Access the app screen by swiping up the screen while on the Home screen.
2. While in the app screen, tap and hold an app icon and select **Add to Home**.

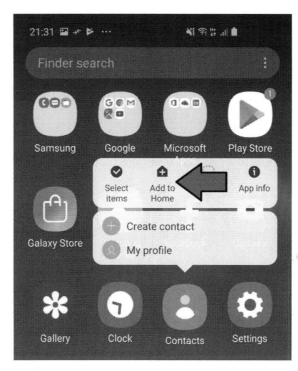

3. To move an app icon to a new location on the Home screen, simply tap, hold and drag it to that location.
4. To remove an app icon from the Home screen, tap and hold the app icon you want to remove, then select **Remove from Home**. Please note that removing an app icon from the home screen does not uninstall the app, it merely removes it from the Home screen.

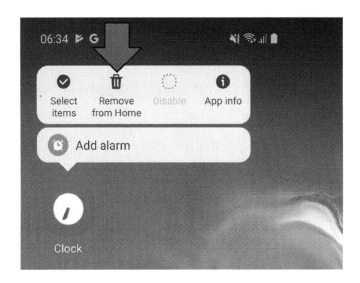

Managing the Home screen widget

A widget is a small item that allows you to control an app in a special way. Widgets display information and allow users to carry out some certain tasks without going into the apps.

To add a widget to a Home screen:

1. While on the Home screen, place two fingers on the screen, then move them closer, or tap and hold an empty space on the Home screen. To go to the Home screen from any screen, press the Home button ⬜ .

2. Tap on **Widgets** located at the bottom of the screen.

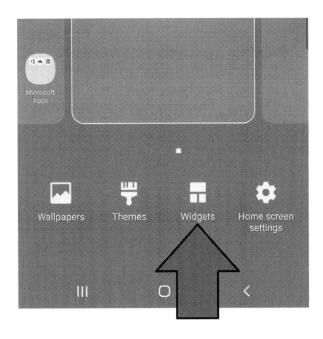

3. Swipe left or right to see the available widgets.

4. Tap a folder to see the widgets inside it.

5. Tap and hold a widget from the list of the widgets that appear, drag it to a Home screen and release it.

6. To move a widget to a new location, tap, hold and drag the widget to the desired location. Tap outside the widget to save the changes.

7. To move a widget to another (Home) screen; tap, hold and drag the widget to the edge of the current screen until the page turns. Repeat this step until you are at the desired Home screen. Lift your finger when you have placed the widget in the desired location.

8. To remove a widget from a Home screen, tap and hold the widget, then select **Remove from Home**. In addition, you can access the widget settings by selecting **Widget settings**.

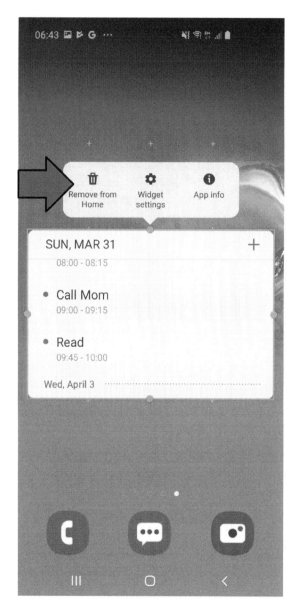

9. To resize a widget, touch and hold, then release the widget. Thereafter, drag the rectangular colored outline to your desired size. Tap outside of the widget to save the changes. *Please note that you may not be able to resize all widgets.*

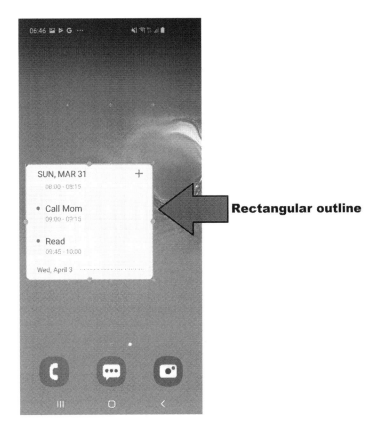

SUN, MAR 31   +
08:00 - 08:15

• Call Mom
09:00 - 09:15

• Read
09:45 - 10:00

Wed, April 3

Rectangular outline

In addition, please note that you may not be able to adjust the size of some widgets vertically.

Managing the Home screen theme

1. While on the Home screen, place two fingers on the screen and move them closer. Alternatively, tap and hold an empty space on the Home screen.

2. Tap **Theme** located at the lower side of the screen and tap **Start.** If prompted, tap **Allow**, if you agree to the request.

3. Choose a theme. *Please note that you may need to agree to Terms and Conditions before you can access themes.*

4. To search for themes, tap the search button located at the top of the screen. Type a search phrase and hit the search icon on the virtual keyboard.

5. To see free themes, scroll down and tap **View all** next to **Popular Free Themes**.

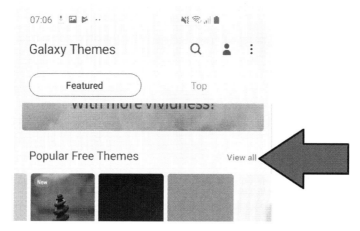

6. When you have seen the theme you like, tap the theme and tap **Download**.

7. Wait for the theme to finish downloading and tap **Apply** (See below).

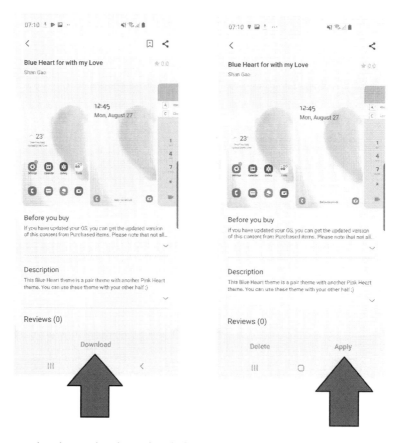

8. To change the theme back to the default one, open themes as described in steps 1 and 2 above. Then tap the default theme and tap **Apply**.

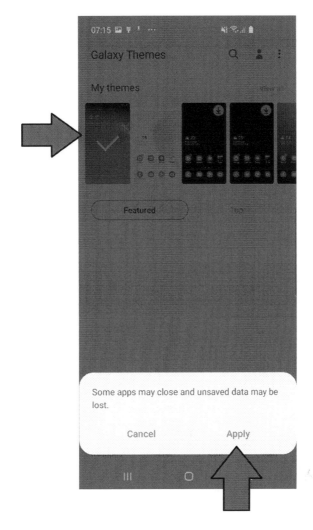

Please note that visual elements such as colors, icons, and wallpapers may change depending on the selected theme.

Managing the Home screen wallpaper

This option allows you to change the wallpaper settings for the Home screen and the locked screen.

1. While on the Home screen, place two fingers on the screen, then move them closer. Alternatively, tap and hold an empty space on the home screen. To go to the home screen from any screen, press the home button ⬜.

2. Tap on **Wallpapers** located at the bottom of the screen.

3. To search for wallpapers, tap the search button located at the top of the screen. Type a search phrase and hit the search icon on the virtual keyboard.

4. To view free wallpapers, scroll down and tap **View all** next to **Popular Free Wallpapers**.

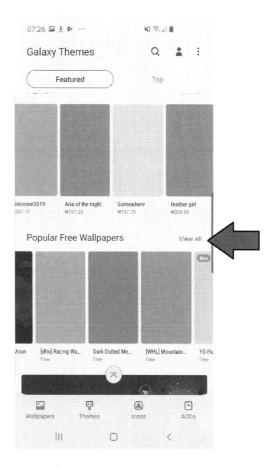

5. When you have seen the wallpaper you like, tap **Download**, then tap **Apply**.

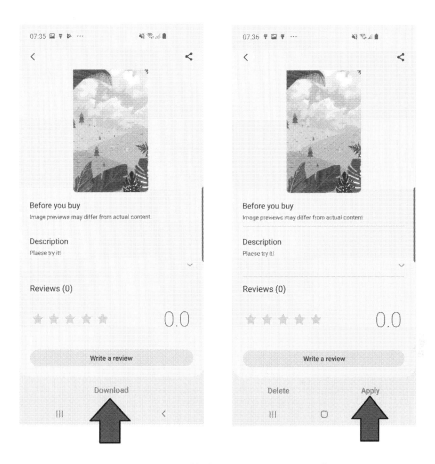

6. Choose whether you want the wallpaper to appear on the **Home screen, Lock screen, or Home and lock screens**.

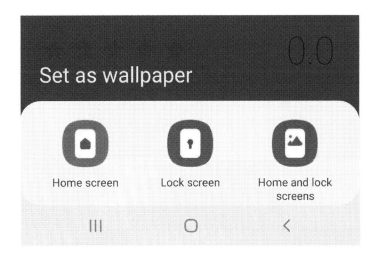

7. Select **Motion Effect**, if you want to give your wallpaper a motion effect. *Motion effect add some animations to your chosen wallpaper.*

Please note that "motion effect" may not be available if you choose "Lock screen" in step 6 above.

8. Tap **Set As Wallpaper.**

Please note that you might be prompted while trying to apply a wallpaper, just read the information shown to you and agree if you like.

What about the screen grid?

The screen grid option allows you to choose the number of app icons that is displayed in a row on your Home screen.

1. While on the Home screen, place two fingers on the screen, then move them closer. Alternatively, tap and hold an empty space on the Home screen.
2. Tap **Home screen settings**.
3. Tap **Home screen grid**.

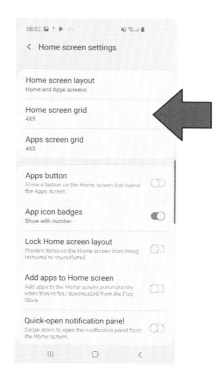

4. Choose a dimension. 4x5 means there are four apps in a row and five apps in a column; 4x6 means there are four apps in a row and six apps in a column; 5x5 means there are five apps in a row and five apps in a column; and 5x6 means there are five apps in a row and six apps in a column.

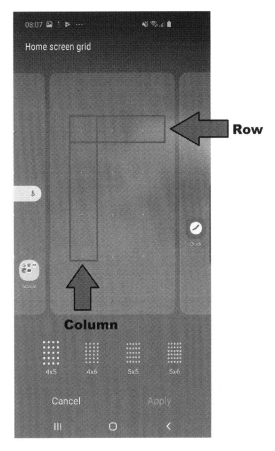

5. When you are done picking a dimension, tap **Apply** (located at the bottom of the screen).

Tip: In addition, you can change the app screen grid by following a similar method. Simply repeat steps 1 and 2 above and tap **Apps screen grid**. Thereafter, choose an option and tap **Apply** to save the changes.

Creating a folder of items/apps on the Home Screen

1. From the Home screen or applications screen, tap and hold an app, then drag and drop it onto another item/app's icon to create a folder.
2. Tap **Enter folder name** and enter a name.
3. To change the color of the folder, tap the color icon ⬤ and select a color.
4. To add another app, tap **Add Apps** located at the bottom of the screen.

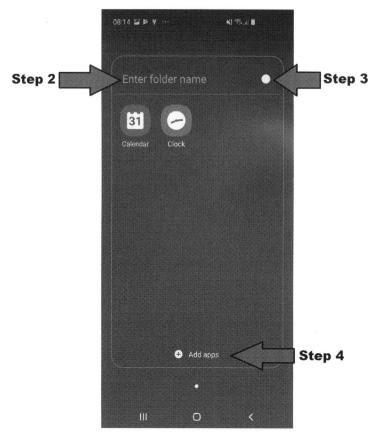

5. When you are done customizing a folder, tap the **Done** button on the virtual keyboard or tap the back icon or both.

6. To remove an app from a folder, tap the folder, then long-tap the app you want to remove and drag it out of the folder.

Please note that the folder is automatically deleted when it remains only one app in the folder.

Accessing and Managing Applications

To open an app:

1. From the Home screen; swipe up from the bottom of the screen to access applications screen.

2. Tap the app of your choice.

3. To go back to the app grid screen, press the back button .

Accessing Recently Opened or Running Applications

1. Tap on the recent button ||| to show the recent apps window. This contains the list of all opened/running apps.

2. While in recent apps window, swipe up an app to close it or tap an app to launch it. To close all opened apps, tap **Close all** located at the bottom of the screen.

Tip: You can lock an app so that it does not get closed when you tap **Close all.** To do this,

tap the recent button  and select an app icon. Then select **Lock apps.**

*Please note that although a locked app is not closed when you tap **CLOSE ALL**, you can still close it by swiping it up.*

Advice: Although Samsung Galaxy S10, S10 Plus or S10e can run many apps at a time, multitasking may cause memory problems or additional power consumption. To avoid these, end all unused programs by closing the apps.

Uninstalling/Deleting an App

If you don't need an app again, you can uninstall it. To do this:

1. From the applications screen, locate the app you want to uninstall. Tap and hold this app, then select **Uninstall**.
2. Tap **OK** to confirm.

Note: Please note that you might not be able to uninstall some of the apps that come preloaded on your device, you might only be able to disable some of them. To disable an app that comes preloaded on your phone, repeat step 1 above and select **Disable**. A disabled app will be removed from the application list and will not be able to perform any action on your phone. To reenable an app, go to **Settings** > **Apps**. Then tap the app you want to enable and select **Enable**.

Managing the applications screen

Selecting Apps

You can select many apps to perform an action on all of them at the same time. To do this:

1. Tap and hold an app and tap **Select items**.

2. Then select all apps you want and choose an option at the top of the screen. If an option appears gray that means you can't use the option. For example, if your selection contains a folder, the **Create folder** icon would appear gray because you can't put a folder inside another folder.

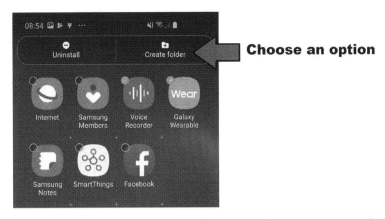

Choose an option

To move all of the selected apps to another part of the screen, tap, hold and drag one app in your selections. In addition, you can drag one of the selected apps up the screen to add them to the Home screen.

Tip: Usually, when there is an app notification, a badge appears on the corresponding app icon. If an app has a badge, you can clear this badge by following the method below.

- Swipe down from the top of the screen to access the notifications screen.

- Dismiss the corresponding notification on the notification screen to clear the badge. You can dismiss a notification by swiping the notification towards right or left. For example, if Google Play store app has a badge, you would dismiss this badge when you dismiss its notification on the notification screen.

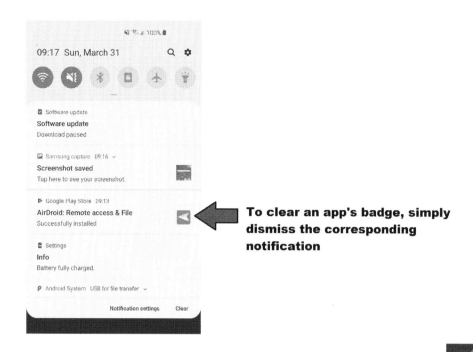

To clear an app's badge, simply dismiss the corresponding notification

Please note that a badge is a notification number displayed on an app icon, e.g.

Tip: To customize *app icon badges* settings, swipe down from the top of the screen and tap settings icon ⚙. Tap the search icon 🔍 and type in **app icon badges** into the search bar located at the top of the screen. The result filters as you type. Tap **app icon badges** from the results that appear.

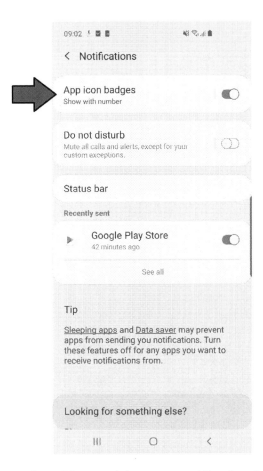

Then select **Show with number**. If you wish to see notification details when you touch and hold an app on the Home screen, select **Show notifications**.

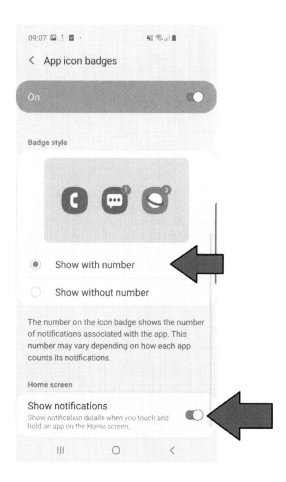

Showing the Apps Button

You can choose to show the Apps button 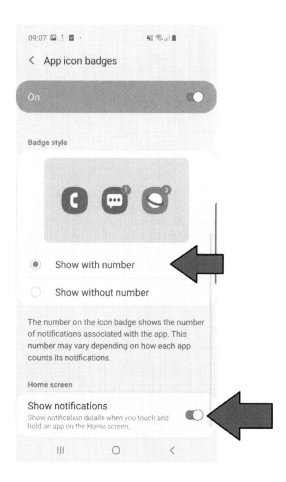 on the Home screen. When you tap the apps button, you would be taken to the applications screen.

To show the apps button:

1. While on the Home screen, swipe up the screen to access the applications screen.

2. Tap the menu icon ⋮ next to the search bar and select **Home screen settings**.

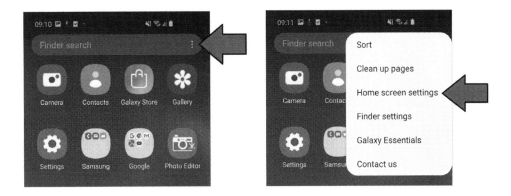

3. Tap **Apps button** to enable this feature.

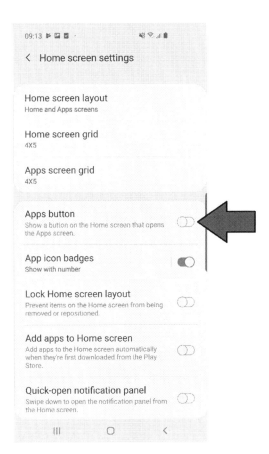

Apps button would appear on the Home screen when enabled. See the picture below.

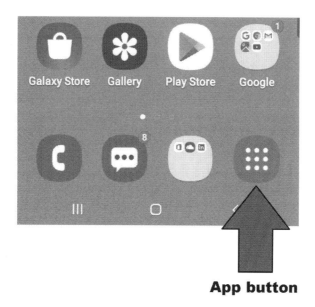

App button

Arranging Applications Alphabetically

1. While on the Home screen, swipe up the screen to access the application screen.

2. Tap the menu icon ⋮ next to the search bar.

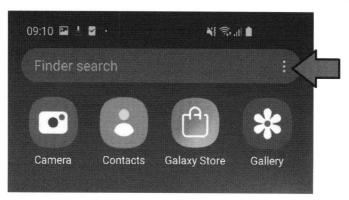

3. Tap **Sort** and choose an option.

Tip: If you choose to arrange your apps/folders alphabetically, the folders would appear first.

Hiding Applications

If you don't want your kids to access sensitive apps on your phone, you can hide them. For example, if you don't want your children to access your shopping app, you can hide it. However, please note that people may still be able to see your hidden apps if they are tech savvy and they know the way.

To hide apps:

1. While on home screen, swipe up the screen to access the applications screen.

2. Tap the menu icon ⋮ next to the search bar and select **Home screen settings**.

3. Scroll down and tap **Hide apps.** Then select the apps you want to hide and tap **APPLY** located at the bottom of the screen.

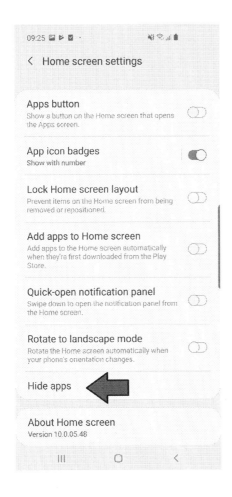

4. To unhide the apps, just repeat the steps 1 to 3 above and deselect the apps you have selected before. Then tap **APPLY** located at the bottom of the screen.

Managing Applications

You can force-stop a misbehaving app. In addition, you can clear cache/data to clear errors in an app or to save phone memory.

To force-stop an app and manage app settings:

1. Swipe down from the top of the screen and tap settings icon ⚙ .
2. Scroll down and tap **Apps**.
3. Tap the app you want to manage.
4. To force-stop an app, tap **Force stop.** Force-stopping an app is useful when an app is misbehaving or when it refuses to close. To access a force-stopped app again, just relaunch the app from the application screen.
5. To clear the cache or data of an app, tap **Storage**, then tap **CLEAR DATA** or **CLEAR CACHE.** *Please note that clearing **data** may cause you to lose settings, files and all other stored information on the app. Only clear the data of an app if you want to start using it as a new app.*

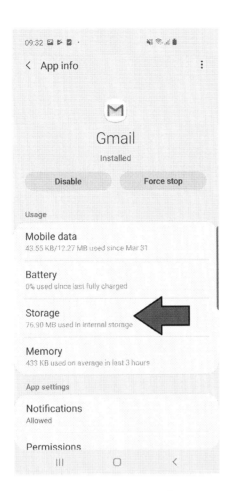 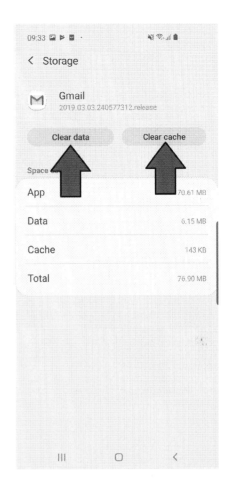

Tip: If you don't see **Clear Data** in step 5 above, then choose **Manage Storage.** When you choose **Manage Storage** option, you should be able to access the Clear Data tab.

6. To manage the notification of an app, tap **Notifications** and choose an option.

7. To manage the permissions you have given to an app, scroll down and tap **Permissions**. Then choose an option.

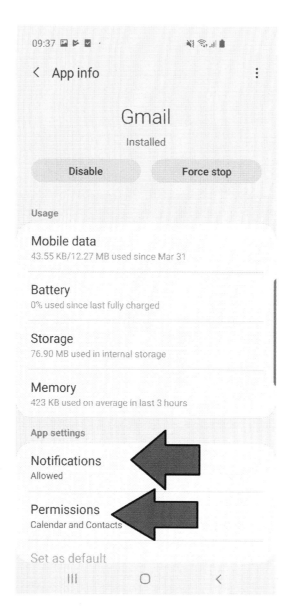

Tip: If an app is disturbing you with notifications and you want to quickly manage notification settings, just swipe down from the top of the screen and tap **Notification settings**. Select **See all**.

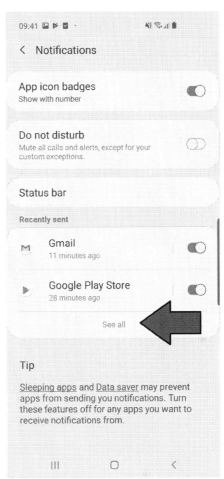

Then use the status switch next to each app to block/allow their notifications. To learn more about phone notifications, see page 93.

Tip: Are there any confidential documents, files or items you want to make private so that only you can access them? If yes, do the following to protect them:

Swipe down from the top of the screen and tap **Settings** > **Biometrics and security** > **Secure folder**. Follow the on-screen instructions to complete the process.

Managing the Navigation Bar

The navigation bar is the bar at the bottom of your device screen. This bar comprises back icon, Home icon and recent apps icon. Interestingly, you can hide or unhide this bar. To manage the navigation bar:

1. Swipe down from the top of the screen and tap settings icon .
2. Tap **Display**.
3. Scroll down and select **Navigation bar**.
4. Choose an option from the Navigation bar settings screen.
5. To completely hide the navigation bar, select **Full screen gestures** and then tap the switch next to **Gesture hints** to deactivate it. Please note that "Gesture hints' tab may not appear unless you have selected "Full screen gestures".

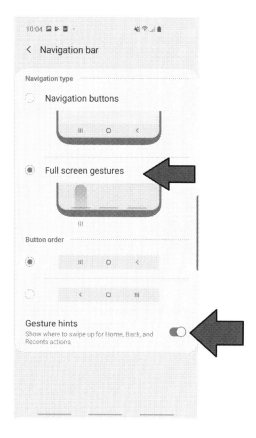

6. To use a navigation button after hiding it, simply swipe up on where the button normally appears.

7. To show the navigation buttons again, repeat steps 1 to 3 and select **Navigation buttons**.

Tip: You can easily enable or disable navigational buttons by swiping down from the top of the screen using two fingers. Then swipe left until you see the navigational button icon. Thereafter, tap it to enable or disable it.

Managing Phone Notifications

Notifications consume battery and it may be a source of disturbance occasionally. To manage notifications:

1. Swipe down from the top of the screen and tap settings icon .

2. Then tap **Notifications**.

3. Tap **See all** found at the bottom of the screen.

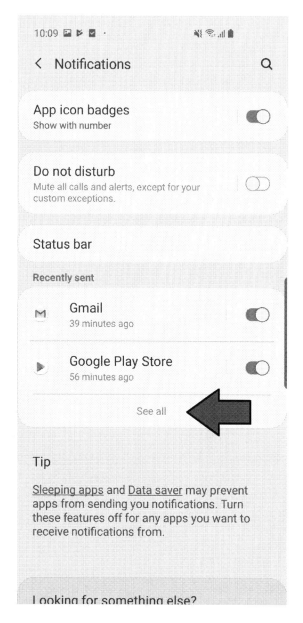

4. Use a status switch to block notification for an individual app.

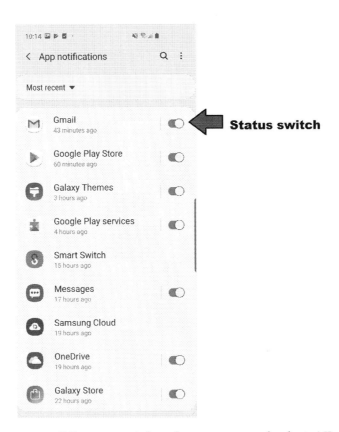

5. To see all apps, tap **Most recent** dropdown menu and select **All**

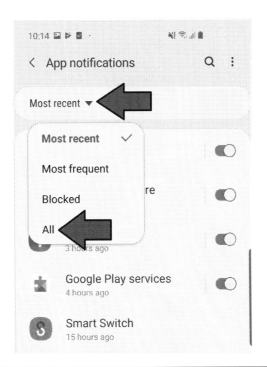

Tip: To manage notification sound on your phone, swipe down from the top of the screen and tap **Settings** 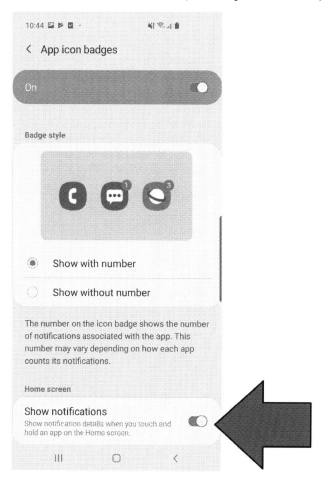 > **Sounds and vibration** > **Notification sounds**. If you are using a dual SIM model, select a SIM. Then select **Silent** if you don't want a notification sound. To change your selection, choose a notification sound.

You should be able to see your notifications at a glance when you touch and hold an app icon on the Home screen.To do this, swipe down from the top of the screen and tap settings icon . Select **Notifications** and then **App icon badges**. Then scroll down and tap the status switch next to **Show notifications** (see the picture below).

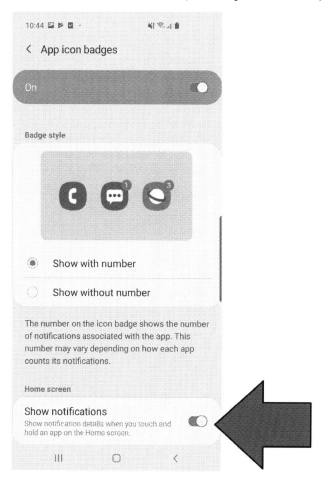

If you do not want to see any form of notification icons/badges or details on your apps screen, tap the status switch next to **ON**.

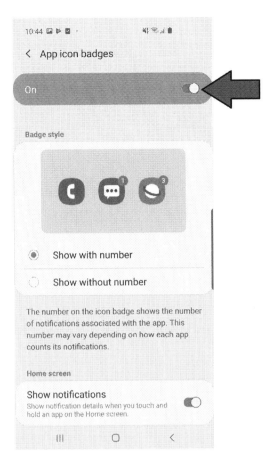

Furthermore, you can quickly view the details of a notification from the quick action menu. To do this, simply swipe down from the top of the screen, tap and hold a notification, then tap **Details**.

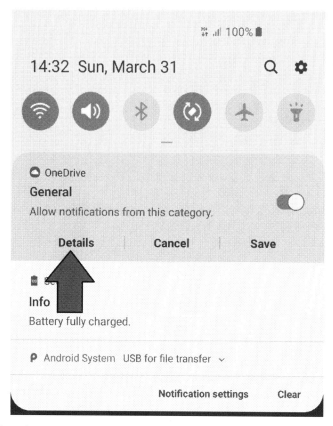

Then select an option from the screen that appears.

Hint: You can turn off all sounds on your phone including sounds from calls, alerts and media. To do this, go to **Settings** > **Accessibility** > **Hearing enhancements** > **Mute all sounds**.

Troubleshooting Tip: If you are not getting notification from an app (for example, if you are not getting notifications from Email app), these are the things to check:

1. Check whether you have not blocked notifications from this app. You can know this by following the steps on page 93-95.

2. Confirm that you have not disabled **Sync** function. To do this, swipe down from the top of the screen with two fingers. Then swipe left and see if **Sync** appears bold. If it appears bold, then it is enabled. Please note that if *Sync* is disabled you may not get some notifications.

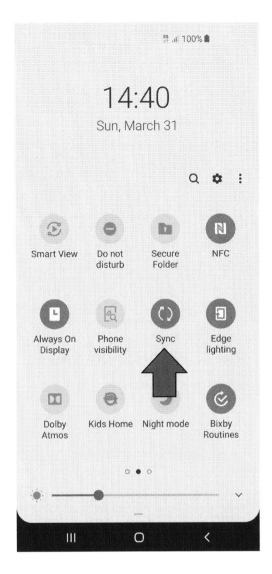

3. If the first two steps above do not work, then make sure your phone is not restricting the app's battery usage. Restricting the battery usage for an app may affect the ability of the app to get sync or use data. To know if an app has a restricted battery usage, go to **Settings** ⚙ > **Apps** > **menu icon** ⋮ (located at the top of the screen) > **Special access** > **Optimize battery usage**. Tap the dropdown menu and select **All**. Locate the app in question and make sure the indicator switch next to it is turned off.

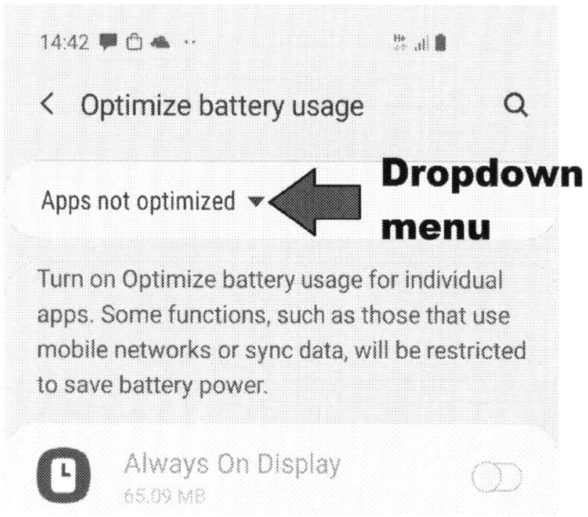

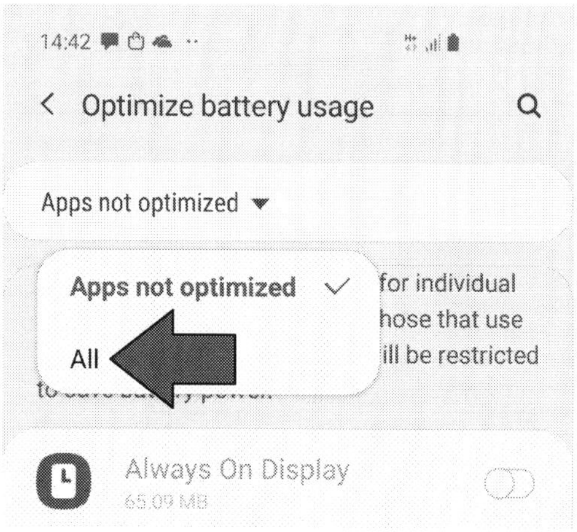

Hint: You could dismiss a notification by swiping down from the top of the screen and then swiping left/right on the notification that you want to dismiss.

Using the Multi Window/Split-Screen Function

Multi window is one of the coolest features of Samsung Galaxy S10, S10 Plus and S10e. Multi window allows you to put two apps side by side. *However, it is important to note that some apps may not support multi window feature.*

Using Multi Window feature:

1. Open an app that supports multi-screen (e.g. phone app).
2. Tap the Recents button 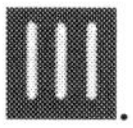.
3. Tap an app icon. In this example we would tap the phone app icon.

4. Select **Open in split screen view**.

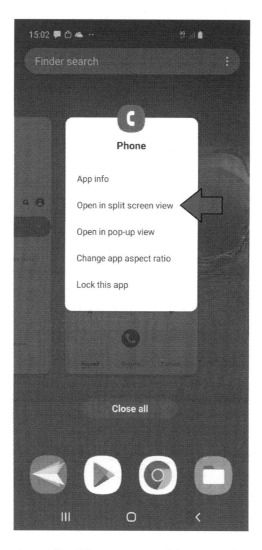

5. The current/selected app (i.e. Phone app in this example) will launch in the upper window and the other recently used apps that support multi window will display below the launched app. Swipe left or right (if necessary) and select the second app.

6. To adjust the size of an app window, tap the middle of the dividing line between the app windows (i.e. the straight line that appears between the two app windows) and drag it up or down. See the picture below.

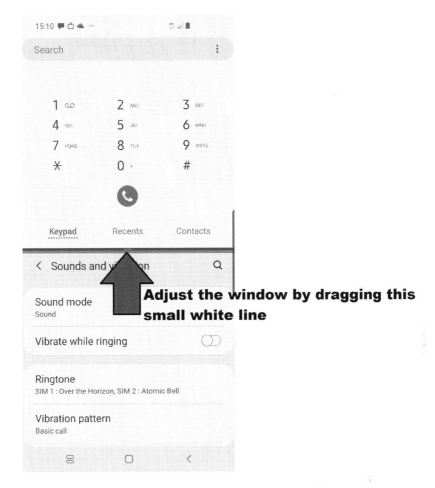

Note that when you drag the bar between the two app windows to the top edge or bottom edge of the screen, the multiwindow would be exited and the current app would be maximized.

7. To close an app opened in split-screen, tap the split-screen icon and swipe up the thumbnail of the app you want to close.

8. To open another app in split-screen, tap the split-screen icon , and select an app.

9. To exit multi window (split-screen) view, tap the split-screen icon (located at the bottom of the screen) and then select the **X** icon.

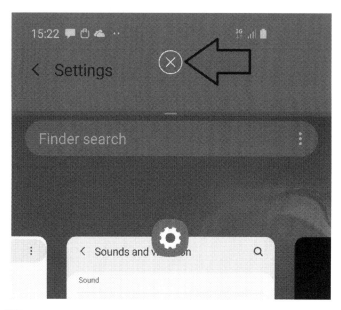

Using the Pop-up View

You can open an app in Pop-up view so that it appears like a small pop-up window on the screen. To do this:

1. Open the app you want to open in pop-up view.

2. Tap the Recents button ▦.

3. Tap the app icon of the app you want to open in pop-up view. In this example, we would tap the phone app icon.

4. Select **Open in pop-up view**.

5. Tap [icon] to minimize the app window to a small icon. This small icon can be dragged from one part of the screen to another when you tap, hold and move it. To expand the small icon, simply tap it.

6. Tap [icon] to maximize the window to a full screen.

7. To adjust the transparency of the pop-up window, click on [icon]. Then use the slider that appears to adjust the transparency.

8. To move the pop-up window to other part of the screen, tap and hold the upper part of the pop-up window (next to the outline i.e. border) then drag it to where you want.

9. To resize the pop-up window, tap, hold and move the outline (border) as you wish.

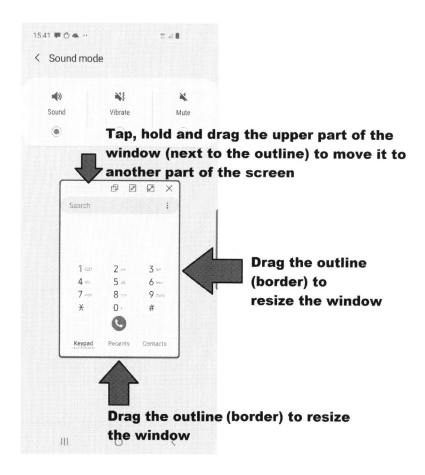

10. Tap the **X** icon on the pop-up window to close it.

Understanding the Quick Settings menu

The Quick settings panel (menu) provides a quick access to device functions such as Wi-Fi, allowing you to quickly turn them on or off. You access Quick settings panel when you swipe down from the top of the screen.

Tip: The app icon that is currently active in Quick settings panel will appear bold, so if you want to know whether you have enabled a feature or not, just check its boldness. For example, if you want to know if Bluetooth is on, swipe down from the top of the screen and see if the Bluetooth icon appears bold.

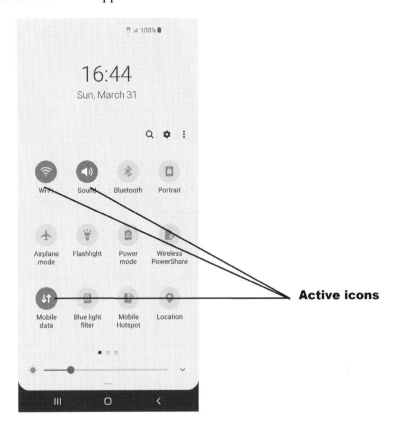

To view additional Quick settings:

1. Swipe down from the top of the screen to display the Quick settings and Notification panel.

2. Drag down the dash icon (—) to see more icons (see the picture below).

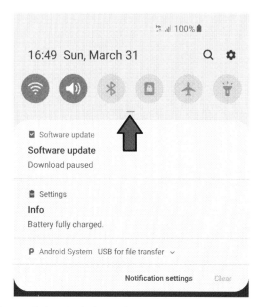

Tip: To have a robust view of the Quick settings panel icons, swipe down from the top of the screen using two fingers.

To customize the Quick settings panel icons:

1. Swipe down from the top of the screen using two fingers.

2. Tap the menu icon ⋮ located at the top of the screen.

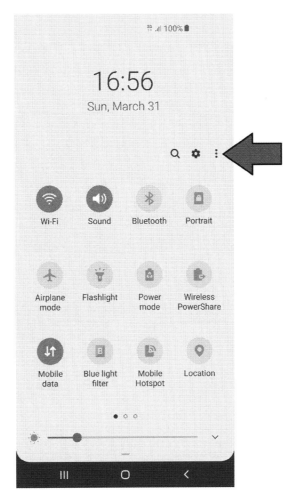

3. Tap **Button order.**

4. Tap, hold and drag any of the icons to change their positions.

5. To add an app to the Quick settings panel, drag the app from upper section of the screen (the gray area) to the lower section of the screen.

6. To remove an icon from the Quick settings panel, drag the app icon to the upper section of the screen (the gray area).

Gray area containing inactive icons

White area containing active icons

8. Tap **Done** located at the bottom of the screen to save the changes.

9. To restore the icons' arrangement to the default arrangement, tap **Reset** and tap **Done.**

Tip: To change the number of app icons that appear in a row/column in Quick settings menu, repeat steps 1 and 2 above. Then select **Button grid** and choose an option. Select **OK** to save the changes.

Customizing Your Phone

You can get more done with your phone by customizing it to match your preference.

Changing Your Phone Language

1. Swipe down from the top of the screen and select settings icon . Then scroll down and tap **General management.**

2. Tap **Language and input.**

3. Tap **Language**.

4. Tap **Add language**.

5. If you want to access a more robust list of languages, tap the menu icon ⋮ and tap **All languages**.

6. Select a language from the list. If your chosen language is spoken in more than one country/region, select a country/region for your chosen language.

7. Using the icon ⌃⌄ next to a language, tap and drag your preferred language to the number one position in the language list. Then tap **Apply** to set the language (in number one position) as the default language.

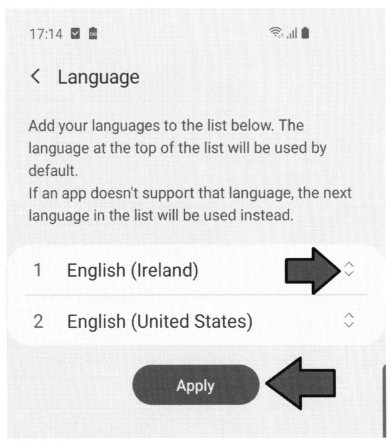

8. To delete a language, tap **Remove** located at the top of the screen and tap the language you want to delete. Then select **Remove** and tap **Remove** again. See below for details.

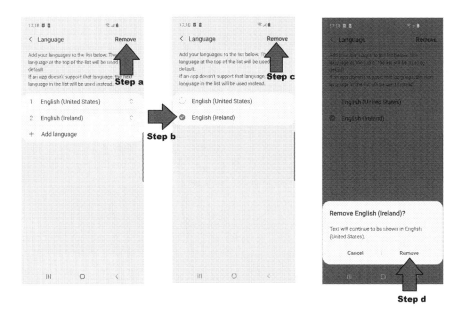

Selecting the Default Keyboard

1. Swipe down from the top of the screen and select settings icon ⚙. Then scroll down and tap **General management**.

2. Tap **Language and input.**

3. Tap **Default Keyboard** and choose a keyboard. Please note that if you have not downloaded extra keyboards from Google Play Store, you may see only one keyboard.

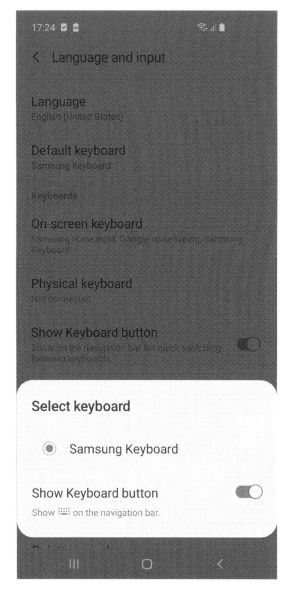

I would recommend that you go to Google Play Store to download more keyboard(s). Just open Google Play Store app and search for **Keyboard.** Then choose a keyboard from the options that appear. After you have downloaded and installed a keyboard, then perform the following actions:

1. Swipe down from the top of the screen and select settings icon ⚙. Then scroll down and tap **General management.**
2. Tap **Language and input.**

3. Tap **On-screen keyboard**

4. Tap **Manage keyboards**. See the picture below.

5. Tap the status switch next to the keyboard you just installed to enable it. In this case, I have just downloaded and installed **SwiftKey Keyboard** from Google Play store.

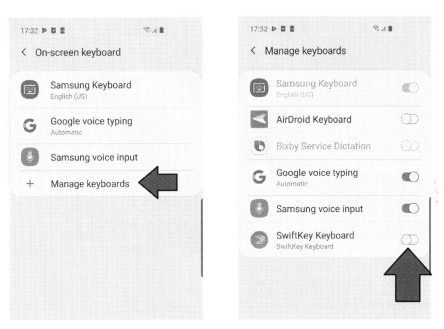

6. Your device would display a cautionary note, read this note and tap **OK** if you agree.

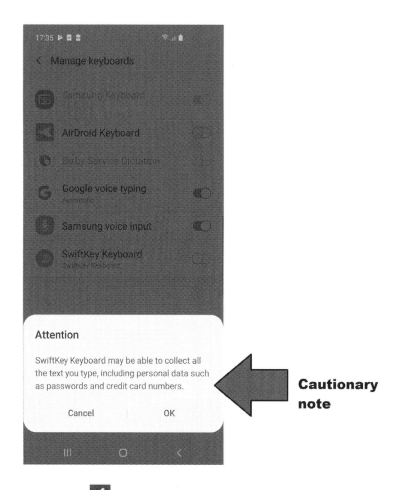

7. Tap the back button 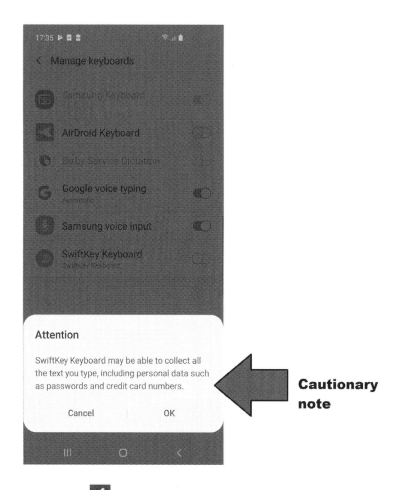 until you see **Language and Input** screen. Then tap **Default keyboard** and choose an option.

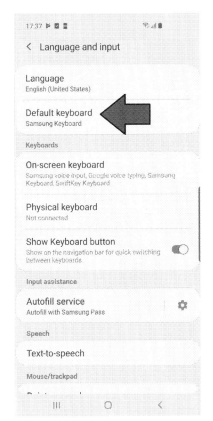
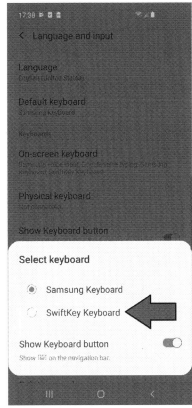

Tip: Your device comes preloaded with Samsung keyboard. To customize this keyboard to your taste, swipe down from the top of the screen and tap settings icon > **General management** > **Language and input** > **On-Screen Keyboard** > **Samsung keyboard.** Then tap any of the on-screen options. I would advise that you go through these options serially to have the best keyboard experience.

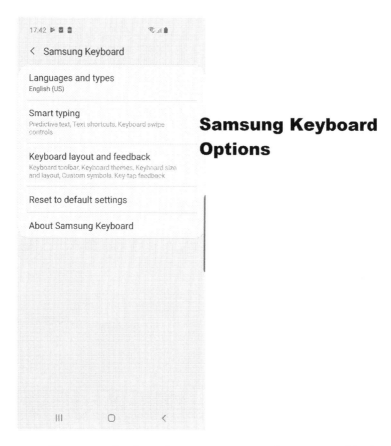

Samsung Keyboard Options

In addition, you can allow your keyboard to support more languages. To do this, swipe

down from the top of the screen and tap settings icon 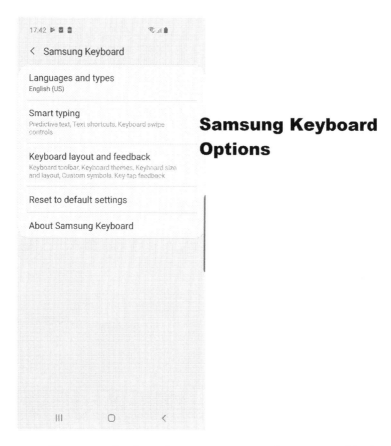 > **General management >**
Language and input > On-Screen Keyboard > Samsung keyboard > Languages and
types > Manage input languages. Then tap the status switch next to all the languages you
want the keyboard to support.

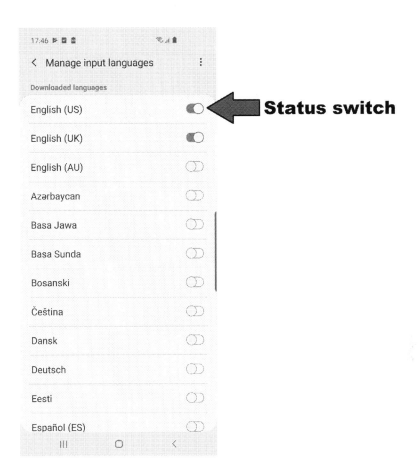

Status switch

To change your keyboard language to any of the one selected above, swipe the space bar key on the virtual keyboard to right or left until you see the language of your choice.

Swipe this to right or left

Set the Current Time and Date

Your device is built to update its time automatically, but you may need to manually set your time for one reason or the other. To manually set the time and date:

1. Swipe down from the top of the screen and select settings icon ⚙. Then scroll down and tap **General management**.
2. Tap **Date and time.**
3. To ensure that the time on your device is updated automatically, enable the status switch next to **Automatic date and time.** Please note that when this status switch is enabled, it would appear bold.
4. To set the time on your device manually or prevent your device from updating the time automatically, disable the status switch next to **Automatic date and time**, then edit the time and date as you desire.
5. To manage the time zone settings, disable the status switch next to **Automatic date and time**, then tap **Select time zone.**

6. To use a 24 hours' time setting for your device, enable the status switch next to **Use 24-hour format**.

Tip: When the status switch is on, it would appear bold.

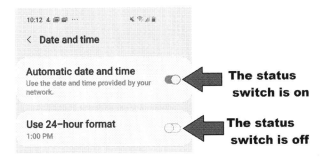

Controlling Sounds and Vibrations

1. Swipe down from the top of the screen and select settings icon .

2. Tap **Sounds and vibration** and tap an option.

3. For example, to mute the sound on your phone, tap **Sound mode**, then tap **Mute**.

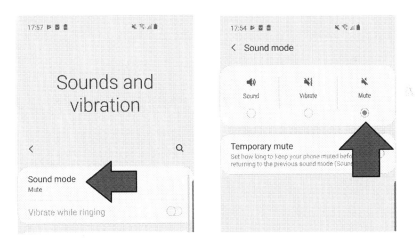

To mute your phone temporarily, tap the switch next to **Temporary mute**. Then select **Mute duration**.

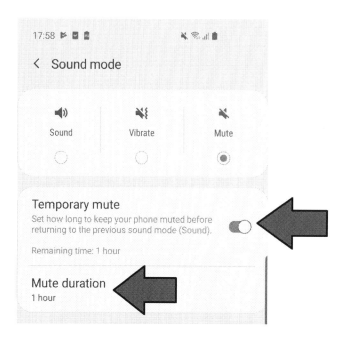

Adjusting the Volume of Your Phone

To adjust the volume of your phone, press the **Volume key**. The volume key is the long key located at the left side of your phone (when the phone is facing you).

Adjusting the Brightness of the Display

1. Swipe down from the top of the screen using two fingers. Then drag the slider under the Quick action panel icons to adjust the brightness.

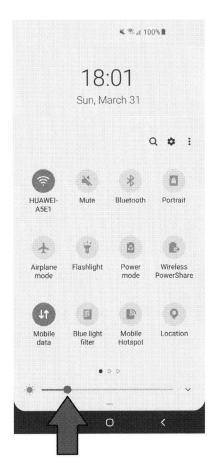

Tip: The brightness level of the display will affect how quickly the device consumes battery power. I would advise that you turn it reasonably low if you are very concerned about saving your battery. In addition, using your phone on high brightness for a long time may strain your eyes.

In addition, to enable adaptive brightness (so that your phone adjusts its brightness based on your usage/lighting conditions), tap the dropdown arrow ∨. Then tap the switch next to **Adaptive brightness**.

Setting a Screen Lock Password or PIN

You can lock your phone by activating the screen lock feature.

Note: Once you set a screen lock, your phone will require an unlock code each time you turn it on or unlock the touch screen.

1. Swipe down from the top of the screen and tap the settings icon .
2. Tap **Lock screen** and tap **Screen lock type**.
3. Tap a screen lock type you like.
4. If you choose **Password** or **PIN**, then enter the **password/PIN** you desire and follow the on-screen instructions to complete the setup. In addition, you may choose **Pattern** or **Swipe.** If you don't want a lock screen, tap **None**.

Tip: You may also use your fingerprint or face to unlock your phone. More on this on page 136-143.

Adjusting Font Size/Style on Your Phone

You can change the font on your phone to a bigger or smaller font by following the steps below:

1. Swipe down from the top of the screen and tap settings icon .
2. Tap **Display**.
3. Select **Font size and style**.
4. To adjust the font size, drag the slider next to **Font Size**. You would see the preview of font size at the upper part of the screen.
5. To change the font style, select a font under the **Font Style** tab.
6. To make the font appear boldened, tap **Bold font**. Boldening the font make it easier to see.

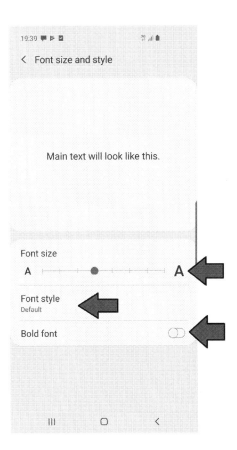

Tip: If you have a senior that has a problem seeing what is on the screen, you could increase the font size using the method above.

Changing the Display Size

You can change the display on your phone to a bigger or smaller display. When the display is bigger, the items on the screen appear bigger. When the display is smaller, the items on the screen appear smaller. To change the display size, follow the steps below:

1. Swipe down from the top of the screen and tap settings icon .
2. Tap **Display**.
3. Select **Screen zoom**
4. To adjust the display size, drag the slider next to **Screen zoom**. You would see the preview of the display size at the upper part of the screen.

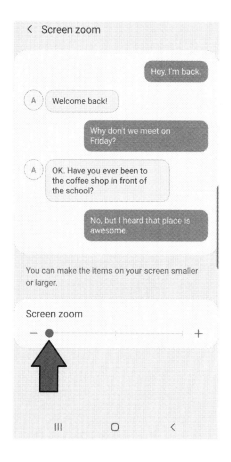

Smart Lock

Smart lock allows you to lock your device in a special way. This feature allows you to quickly lock and unlock your phone.

To use smart lock:

1. Swipe down from the top of the screen and select settings icon .
2. Tap **Lock screen**.
3. If you have not set up a secure lock before, tap **Screen lock type**, choose a PIN and follow the on-screen instructions to set up this lock type. Please skip this step if you have already set up a secure lock.
4. Tap **Smart Lock.** You would only be able to select Smart Lock after you have set up a screen lock type.

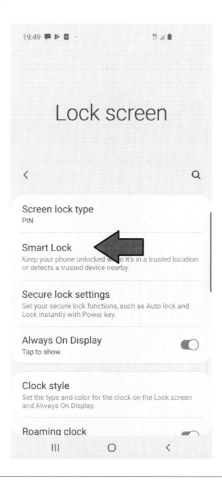

5. Enter your screen lock information and tap **Next**.

6. Read the onscreen instructions and select **Got It**.

7. Pick an option on the screen (the options include **On-body detection**, **Trusted places**, **Trusted devices** and **Voice Match.**) Then follow the on-screen instructions to complete the setup.

To remove or deactivate a smart lock option:

1. Repeat steps 1 to 4 above.

2. Enter your unlock information and then pick a smart lock type.

3. Tap an option corresponding to what you want to do. For example, to remove "Trusted places," tap the current address/place and select **Delete** or **Edit Address** (located at the bottom of the screen).

Note: Please note that using smart lock may allow a third party to easily access your phone. For example, if you set up "trusted places", your phone might unlock while in these places (or around them) even when you don't want it to unlock.

In addition, On-body detection can't distinguish between you and someone else. This means if someone else takes your phone while it is unlocked, the person might be able to access your data because the phone might remain unlocked.

Tip: You can use **Trusted places** option to automatically unlock your phone while at home. All you need to do to achieve this is to set up your home as a trusted place.

In addition, to use "Trusted places", you might need to enable location (if you have not done so).

To activate location services:

1. Swipe down from the top of the screen and select the settings icon .

2. Tap **Biometrics and security**.

3. Tap **Location**.

4. Tap the status switch under **Location** to enable it.

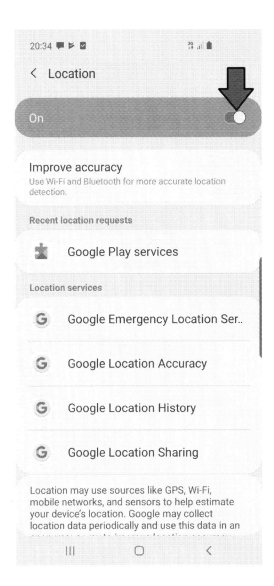

Entering a text

You can enter a text by selecting characters on the virtual keypad or by speaking words into the microphone using a voice command app.

To enter a text:

1. Enter a text by selecting the corresponding letters, symbols or numbers.
2. You can use any of the following keys:

Please note that the on-screen keyboard on your phone may be different from the one shown below. This is because the on-screen keyboard you see depends on the text input field you are working on. The one shown below is the one you should see when you want to compose a text message.

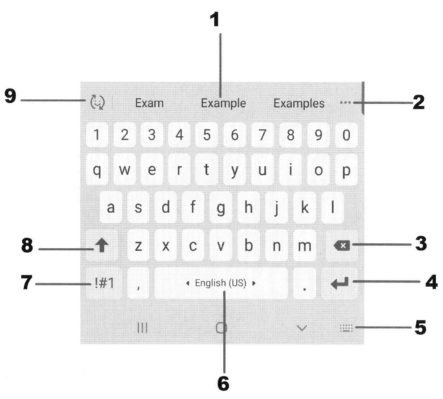

Number	Function
1.	**Predictive text bar** **Tip**: Your phone has an auto replace feature and as you type, it will give you text suggestions. The most likely suggestions would appear in blue on the predictive text bar. To use the suggestion that appears in blue (the suggestion that appears at the center), tap the space bar. To use a different suggestion, then tap on your desired suggestion. Please be informed that you can disable this auto replace feature, to do this, please go to page 133.

2.	Tap on this to see more predictive texts or disable the auto replace option.
3.	Clear your input/backspace
4.	Start a new line.
5.	Tap this icon to select a new keyboard type. If you don't want to see this icon again, tap this icon and tap the status switch next to **Show Keyboard button**. To show this icon again, go to **Settings** ⚙ > **General management** and tap **Language and input**. Then tap the status switch next to **Show Keyboard button**.
6.	**Space bar**: You can swipe right or left to switch between input languages. To add keyboard input language, please go to page 118.
7.	Switch between Number/Symbol mode and ABC mode
8.	Change case
9.	**Option tab**: when you tap this button, you will gain access to a list of icons/functions.

Tip: When you tap the option tab ☺ you will gain access to the following:

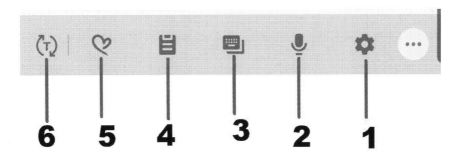

1. **Keyboard settings:** Tap this to access the keyboard settings.
2. **Voice input**: Enter text by voice.

3. **Keyboard options**: Tap this to be able to control the virtual keyboard using one hand. When you tap the "keyboard options' icon 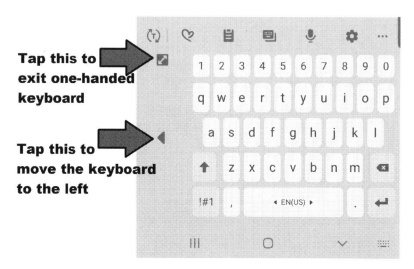 and you then select **One-handed keyboard** button, you will see a keyboard that looks like the one below.

4. **Clipboard:** Tap this to add an item from the clipboard. After using an item on the clipboard, tap the **v** icon (located at the bottom of the screen) to exit.

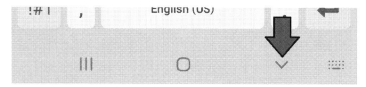

5. **Live message**: Tap this write an animated message.
6. **Option button:** Tap this to switch to predictive texts.

If you select any of the icons described above and you wish to deselect it so as to show the virtual keyboard, simply tap the icon again.

Tip: To learn how to manage the on-screen keyboard, please see the tip on page 117. When you select two or more languages, you can switch between the input languages by swiping to the left or right on the spacebar key.

Hint: By default, you may notice that Samsung automatically replaces your typed word with another one (a corrected one) when you press the space bar. While this option is cool, it may be unwanted sometimes, to disable this function, go to **Settings** ⚙ **> General management > Language and input > On-Screen Keyboard > Samsung keyboard > Smart typing > Auto replace.** Then tap the status switch next to **English** (or your default language) to disable it.

Alternatively, you may disable auto replace by tapping the three dots icon on the virtual keyboard. Then tap the status switch next to **Auto replace**.

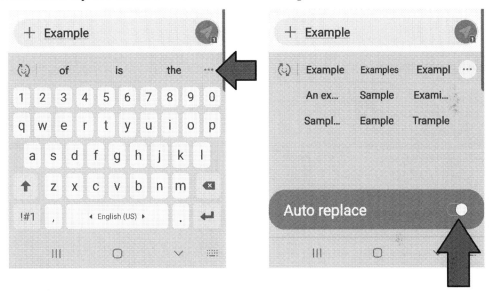

Copy and Paste a Text

While entering or reading a text, you can use the copy and paste options. To do this:

1. Tap and hold a word to display copy options. The icons below will show up after selecting a text or texts.

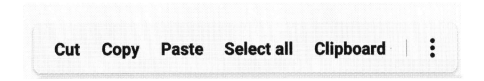

2. Drag  or ![icon] to select more texts.

3. Select **Copy** icon to copy or select **Cut** icon to cut the text onto the clipboard.

4. In another application or where you want to paste the text, tap and hold the text input field.

5. Select **Paste** icon to insert the text from the clipboard into the text input field. You can also tap **Clipboard** to access the clipboard for more paste options. If you can't see "Clipboard", tap the more icon ⋮ and then select "Clipboard".

Using the Voice Typing

1. Tap the option tab ☺ and select 🎤.

2. Say your texts. Your device types as you speak. If you are using voice typing for the first time, please follow the onscreen instructions to set it up.

3. To pause the voice typing, tap .

4. To manage the voice typing option, swipe down from the top of the screen and tap

   Settings ⚙ > **General management** > **Language and input**. Tap **On-Screen keyboard** and tap **Samsung voice input**.

5. To delete, tap the backspace button ⌫ .

6. To exit the voice typing, tap the V-shape icon ⌄ (located at the bottom of the screen).

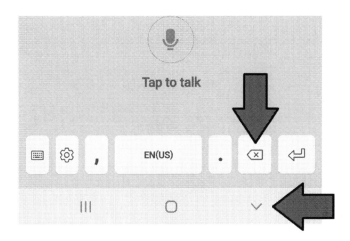

Using The Special Features

Samsung Galaxy S10, S10 Plus and S10e come with special features that make it distinct. I will now explain how to use these features.

Using the Fingerprint Feature

One of the cool features on Samsung Galaxy S10, S10 Plus and S10e is the fingerprint scanner. This allows you to unlock applications without entering boring passwords.

Tip: You can use your biometrics to unlock websites and apps. To learn how to get started, please go to page 220-223.

Registering your Fingerprint

Before you can start using your fingerprint on the device, you will need to first register your fingerprint. You have the chance of registering multiple fingerprints. In addition, you also have the option of registering a password as a backup.

To do this:

1. Swipe down from the top of the screen and select the settings icon 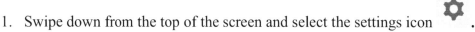 .
2. Tap **Biometrics and security**.
3. Tap **Fingerprints**.
4. Enter your lock screen information. You may need to set up one, if you have not done so before.
5. Read the on-screen tips and tap **Continue**.
6. Tap an alternative lock method and follow the prompts. You will need this alternative lock method in some occasions. If you have set a lock screen before, then you just need to enter the lock PIN/Password.
7. If you are using Samsung Galaxy S10/S10 Plus, place one of your fingers on the fingerprint reader located at the bottom of the screen, then lift it when the fingerprint is detected and read. You may need to repeat this several times. Note

that you might need to press the fingerprint sensor a little harder to get your fingerprint registered.

8. If you are using Samsung Galaxy S10e, place one of your fingers on the fingerprint reader located on the power button, then lift it when the fingerprint is detected and read. You may need to repeat this several times.

9. To add another fingerprint, tap **Add** and follow the prompts.

10. When you are done adding your fingerprints, tap **Done.**

Renaming Fingerprints

1. Swipe down from the top of the screen and select settings icon .

2. Tap **Biometrics and security**.

3. Tap **Fingerprints**.

4. Unlock the screen using the preset screen lock method and tap **Done/Next**.

5. Tap the fingerprint you want to rename. For example, tap **Fingerprint 1.**

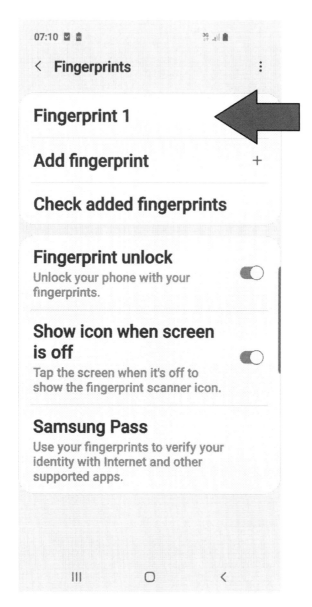

6. Enter a new name and tap **Save**.

Tip: When renaming your fingerprint, make sure you use the name of the finger you registered. For example, you can use the name **Index finger** or **Middle finger**. This prevents unnecessary confusion.

Deleting Fingerprints

1. Swipe down from the top of the screen and select the settings icon   .
2. Tap **Biometrics and security**.
3. Tap **Fingerprints**.
4. Unlock the screen using the preset screen lock method and tap **Done/Next**.
5. Touch and hold the fingerprint you want to delete and tap **Remove**.

Setting a Screen Lock with Fingerprint

You can lock the screen with your fingerprint instead of using a pattern, PIN or password.

1. Swipe down from the top of the screen and select settings icon   .
2. Tap **Lock screen**.
3. Tap **Screen lock type**.
4. Unlock the screen using the preset screen lock method and tap **Next/Done**.
5. Tap the status switch next to **Fingerprint.**

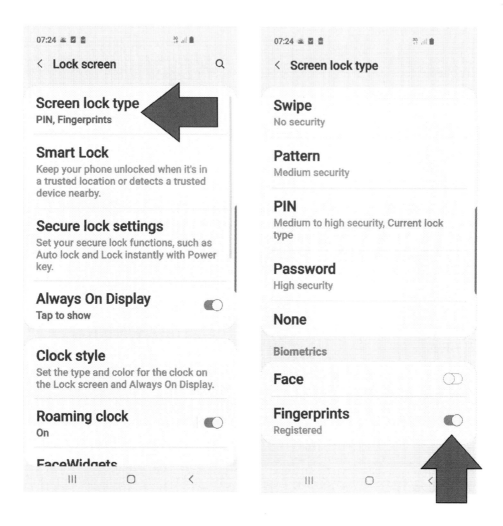

Using Fingerprints to Sign In to Accounts

Apart from using your fingerprint to unlock your device, you can also use it to access online features.

1. Swipe down from the top of the screen and select settings icon .
2. Tap **Biometrics and security**.
3. Tap **Fingerprints**. Unlock the screen using the preset screen lock method, then do any of the following:

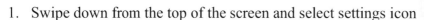

a. Tap **Samsung Pass** to access your online accounts/apps using your fingerprint. To get started with this feature, just tap Samsung Pass and follow the prompts.

b. Tap **Samsung Pay** to use your fingerprint for secured and fast payments with the Samsung Pay app. To get started with this feature, just tap Samsung Pay and follow the prompts. Samsung Pay may not be available in some locations in the world.

c. Tap the switch next to **Fingerprint unlock** to enable or disable fingerprint security.

Tip: If you are using Galaxy S10/S10 Plus, you could show the fingerprint icon when the screen is off. This allow you to know the exact location of the fingerprint reader. To do this, go to **Settings** > **Biometrics and security** > **Fingerprints** > **Show icon when screen is off**.

Troubleshooting the Fingerprint Scanner

If the fingerprint scanner is not responding, try any of the following:

1. If you are using a screen protector, make sure it is not preventing proper communication with the fingerprint reader on Galaxy S10/S10 Plus.

2. Ensure that you are not using the tip of your fingerprint. Make sure to cover the entire Fingerprint reader with your finger.

3. If your finger has scars, try using another finger. This is because your device may not recognize fingerprints that are affected by wrinkles or scars.

4. Ensure the finger you registered with is used.

5. Make sure that your finger and the surface of the fingerprint scanner are clean and dry.

Face Scan

Face scan allow you to unlock your phone with your face. Please note that it appears fingerprint is more secure than face scan.

To use face scan:

1. Swipe down from the top of the screen and select the settings icon .
2. Tap **Biometrics and security**.
3. Tap **Face recognition**. You may need to setup an alternative lock screen method or enter your lock screen information if you have already setup a lock screen.
4. Read the on-screen information and tap **Continue**.
5. Then carefully follow the onscreen instructions to set up face scan.
6. On the Face scan settings page, tap an option to enable/disable it. To know what each option stands for, read the information under the option. Tap **Ok** when you are done.

7. To remove your face data, tap **Remove face data** and select **Remove**.

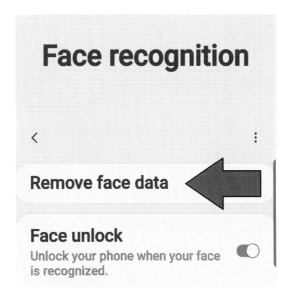

Water Resistance

Another feature that makes Samsung Galaxy S10, S10 Plus and S10e unique is the water resistivity. You don't have to worry about your phone getting wet when you are drenched by the rain or inside a bathroom. To know more about water resistivity, see page 40-41.

Wireless PowerShare

Samsung Galaxy S10/S10 Plus and S10e allows you to share power with other devices that support wireless charging. This is a very cool feature. To know more about this feature, please go to page 24-25.

Using the Always On Feature

The Always On feature allows you to display information, such as a clock, calendar, or image, on the screen when it is turned off. Seeing the time even when the screen is off is cool.

To use this feature:

1. Swipe down from the top of the screen and select settings icon .
2. Tap **Lock screen**.
3. Scroll down and tap **Always on display**.

4. Select On/Off switch to enable or disable Always on Display.

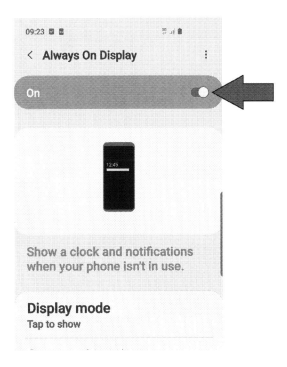

5. Tap Display Mode and choose when you want the **Always on Display** to be active. If you want it to appear at a specific time, select **Show as scheduled** and set the start time and end time.

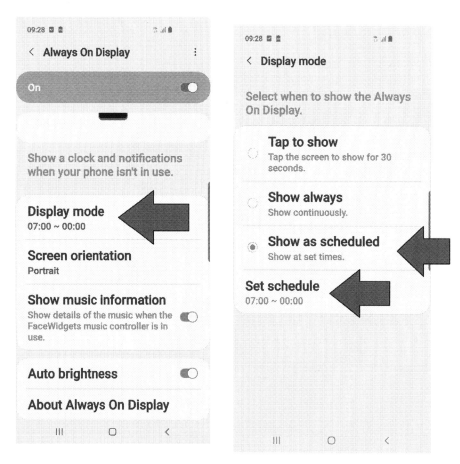

Please note that **Always On Display** may makes your battery drain faster.

Changing the Clock style/Calendar style/Image on "Always On Display"

You can choose the clock style, calendar style, image, or Edge clock to be displayed when "Always On Display" is active. To do this:

1. Swipe down from the top of the screen and select settings icon .
2. Tap **Lock screen**.
3. Tap **Clock style**

4. Select **Always On Display**.

5. Scroll through the available clock style/calendar style/image thumbnails and choose one.

6. Tap **Color** and select color of your choice.

7. Tap **Done** located at the bottom of the screen to effect changes.

Hint: You could also display a clock/calendar on the lock screen. To do this, repeat steps 1 to 3 above. Then choose **Lock screen**. Select an option and tap **Done**.

Tip: You can enable your phone to show you today's schedule and next alarm even when your screen is locked. To do this go to settings 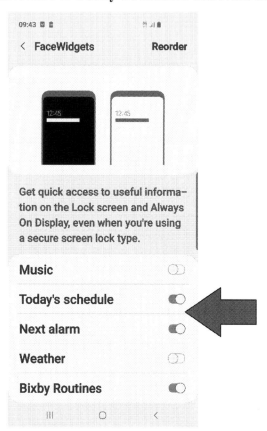 > **Lock screen** > **FaceWidgets**. Then tap the status switches next to **Today's schedule** and **Next alarm.**

To reorder the FaceWidget options, tap on Reorder and use the reordering button ⌄ to change the position of an item. Then tap the back button to save the changes.

Fast Battery Charging

One of the cool features on Samsung Galaxy S10, S10 Plus and S10e is Fast Battery Charging. With this feature, your device can get 50% of battery power in about 45-55 minutes. You can learn how to use this feature by going to page 20-22.

Using the Edge Screen on Samsung Galaxy S10, S10 Plus and S10e

The Edge screen transforms the way you handle your Samsung Galaxy device. Edge panels can be used to access apps, tasks, contacts and more.

Please note that the Edge panel might be disabled by default, to enable Edge panel, go to **Settings** *>* **Display** *>* **Edge Screen**. *Then tap the indicator switch next to* **Edge panels**.

To access the Edge panel:

1. Drag the Edge panel handle located at the edge of the screen. To access more Edge items, swipe again from the edge of the screen. If you are using the Edge panel for the first time, follow the onscreen instructions to get started.

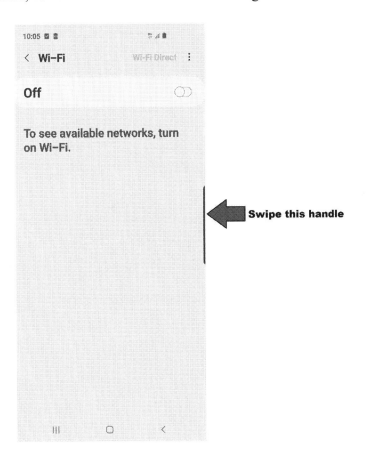

2. To access Edge panel settings, tap the settings icon  located at the bottom of the screen (this settings icon appears while viewing the Edge options).

Using the Edge Panel

The Edge Panel allows you to use the Edge screen in a special way. To manage the Edge panel:

1. Swipe down from the top of the screen and select the settings icon . Then tap **Display** tab**.**

2. Scroll down and tap **Edge Screen**.

3. Tap **Edge Panels**.

4. To download exciting panels, tap the menu icon (located at the top of the screen) and select **Galaxy Store**.

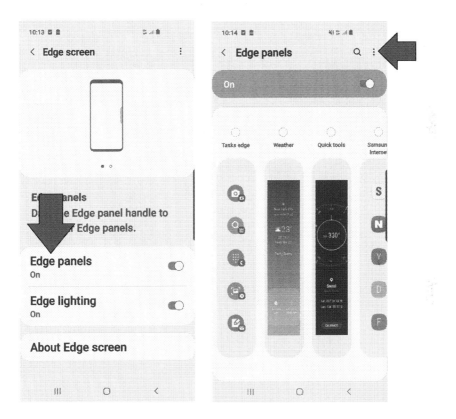

Tap the Edge panel you want to download. Then tap **Install** to download and install your chosen panel. To go back to the Edge panel screen, tap the back button . To see your newly installed panel, navigate to the **Edge Panels** screen and swipe left.

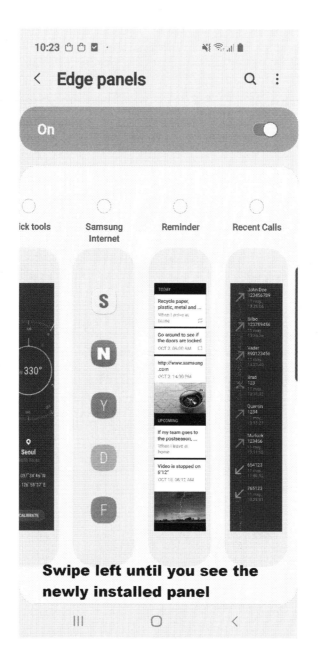

Swipe left until you see the newly installed panel

5. To uninstall an Edge panel that you don't like, tap the menu icon ⋮ located at the top of the Edge panel's screen and select **Uninstall**. Then select the minus icon (--) located at the top of the panel you want to uninstall. When prompted, tap **OK.** Please note that the uninstall button may not be available if you have not installed any Edge panel from the Edge panel (Galaxy) store.

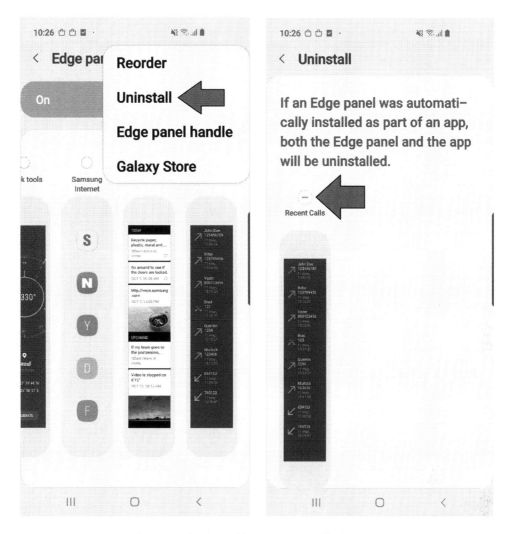

6. There are some Edge panels that allow you to edit them. To edit an editable panel, just tap **EDIT** next to the panel you want to edit. *Please note that you may need to enable a panel before you can edit it. To learn how to enable a panel, please go to step 7.*

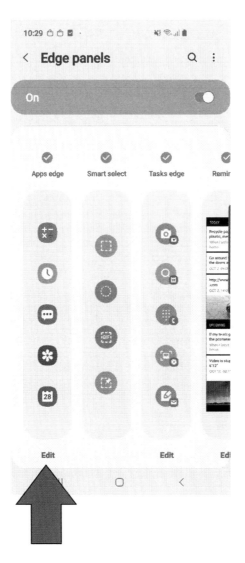

For example, let's say we want to edit **Apps edge**. To add an app to App edge panel, tap and hold the app icon and move it to right side of the screen (see the picture below). To remove an item, tap the minus icon. To rearrange the icons, tap and drag the icon(s) to a new location. See the picture below.

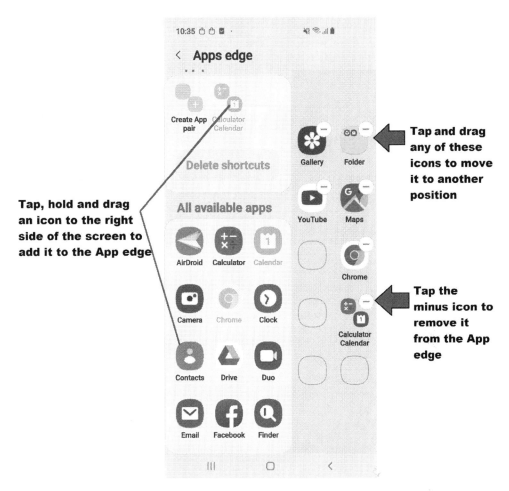

Although, *Apps Edge* has been used in the example above, you can also manage People Edge in a similar way. In addition, please note that there is a maximum number of items you can add to the Edge screen.

To create "app pair" on App edge panel, tap **Create App pair**, tap the two apps you like and tap **DONE** to save the changes.

 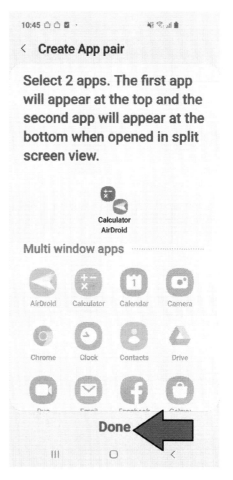

7. To enable an Edge panel or select the Edge panel that you want to see on the Edge screen, simply tap/tick the circle on top of the panel. To disable/remove a panel, simply deselect the circle.

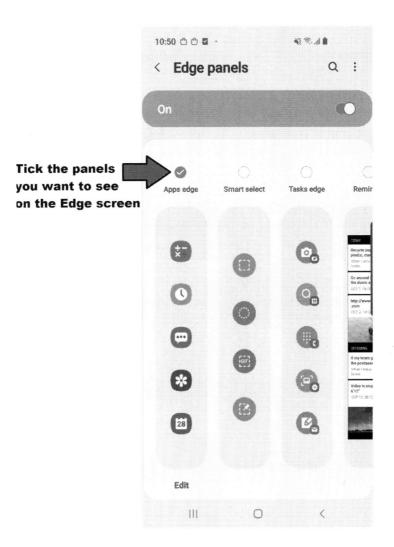

Tick the panels you want to see on the Edge screen

8. To disable Edge panels, tap the status switch next to **ON**. Please note that when you disable the Edge Panel, the Edge handle would disappear.

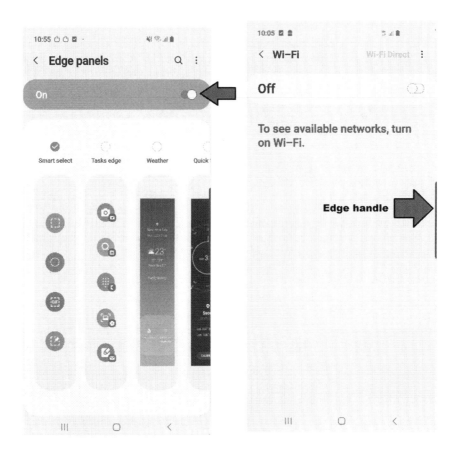

Note: If you download many Edge panels, you may not be able to access all these panels at once on your Edge screen. You may not be able to use more than ten (or less) Edge panels at once. To select the Edge panels that you want to access, simply follow step 7 above.

In addition, to view all the Edge panels you have enabled at once, swipe Edge Panel handle and tap the list icon . Please note that this list icon may not be visible if you have only one panel enabled.

Using the Edge Lighting

This feature allows you to set the Edge screen to light up when you receive calls or notifications.

1. Swipe down from the top of the screen and select settings icon ⚙. Tap **Display** tab.
2. Scroll down and tap **Edge Screen**.
3. Tap **Edge Lighting**.

4. Tap the switch next to **ON**. The switch will appear bold when enabled.

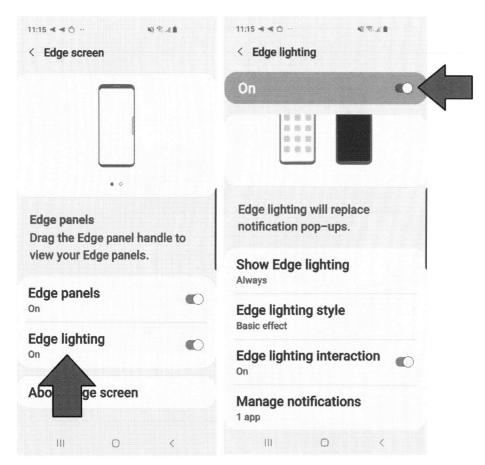

5. Select when to show the Edge lighting by tapping on **Show Edge lighting**. If you want Edge Lighting to be active every time, then select **Always**.

6. Scroll down and tap **Manage notifications** to select those apps that will work with Edge Lighting.

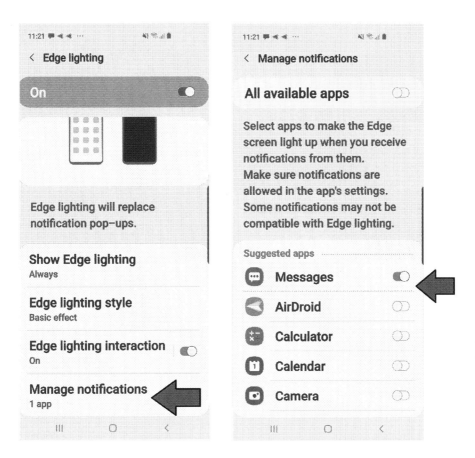

Note: It appears that not all notifications may be received as Edge lighting.

Tip: To customize the color, the size or the transparency of the Edge lighting, tap the **Edge lighting style** and use the on-screen buttons to customize the edge lighting. For example, to change the color of the edge screen lighting, tap **Color** and pick a color. Then tap **Done** to save the changes.

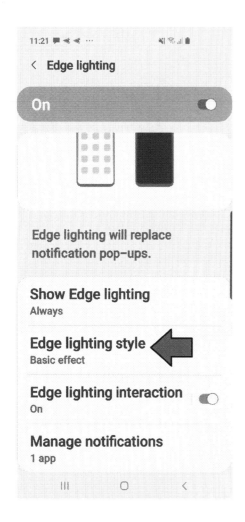

Reordering the Edge Screen Panel

1. Swipe down from the top of the screen and select the settings icon ⚙. Tap **Display** tab.

2. Scroll down and tap **Edge Screen**.

3. Tap **Edge Panels**.

4. Tap the menu ⋮ icon located at the top of the screen and tap **Reorder**.

5. Tap and hold the reorder icon (< >) on an Edge screen panel and drag it to the desired position. Make sure that the panels you use most are the first 3 or 4 panels so that you can access them faster.

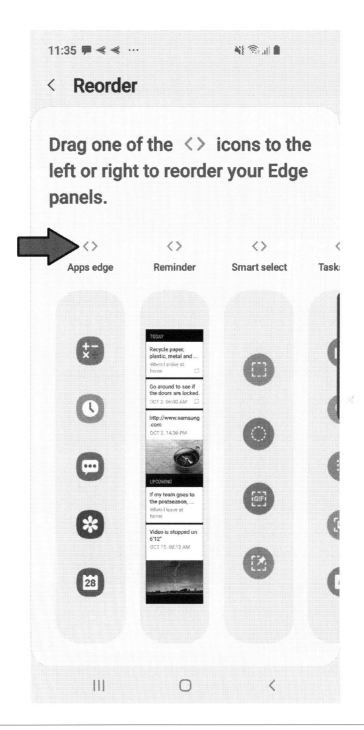

6. Tap back icon ![back] to save the changes.

Managing the Edge Panel Handle Settings/Changing the Edge Panel Location

Edge panel handle settings allows you to change the position of Edge panel and more.

1. Swipe down from the top of the screen and select settings icon ![settings] . Tap **Display** tab.
2. Scroll down and tap **Edge Screen**.
3. Tap **Edge Panels**.
4. Tap the menu icon ![menu] located at the top of the screen and select **Edge panel handle.**
5. Under **Position** tab, tap the side you would like the panel to appear on.
6. To change the transparency of Edge panel, drag the slider under **Transparency.**
7. To change the size of Edge panel, drag the slider under **SIZE**.
8. To move the Edge panel handle to another part of the screen, tap and drag the Edge handle anchor ![anchor] .

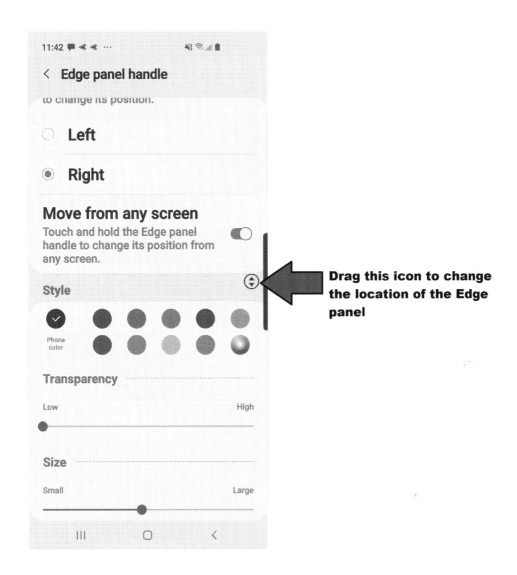

Drag this icon to change the location of the Edge panel

Using People Edge

People Edge gives you the opportunity to quickly access your favorite contacts from Edge Panel.

To manage People Edge:

1. Swipe down from the top of the screen and select settings icon ⚙️. Tap **Display** tab.

2. Scroll down and tap **Edge Screen**.

3. Tap **Edge Panels**.

4. Tap **Edit** under **People edge**. If you can't see the **Edit** button, then **People Edge** is disabled. To enable **People edge**, simply tap/tick the small circle ◯ located on top of this panel.

5. Tap **Select contacts** and select all the contacts you want by tapping them. Please note that you may need to give access to **People Edge** before it can read your contacts. Tap **Done** to save the changes. You should now be able to access the selected contacts when you access the Edge panel.

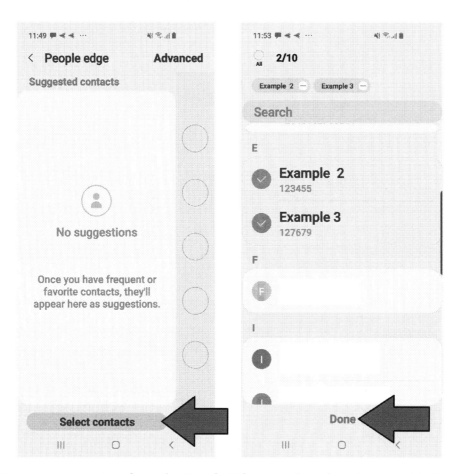

6. To remove a contact from the People Edge, tap the minus icon next to the contact you want to remove.

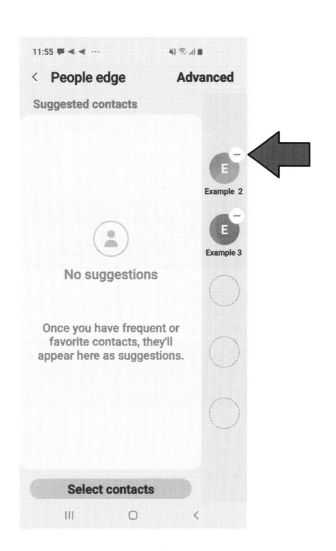

The Bixby

Bixby is a trained virtual assistant that has been built to answer questions and let you interact with your phone in a special way. Bixby is divided into three parts:

1. Bixby Home
2. Bixby Vision
3. Bixby Voice

This section of the guide will show you how to manage Bixby like a pro.

Getting started with Bixby

You would need to setup Bixby when you first start using your device and you would learn how to do that in this section. To setup this voice assistant:

1. Press the Bixby button (the button next to volume button at the side of the phone).

2. If you see a screen telling you to update Bixby, simply tap **UPDATE** and wait for the update to complete.

3. If you are taken to the home screen after the update, press the Bixby button again to open this virtual assistant.

4. Tap next icon .

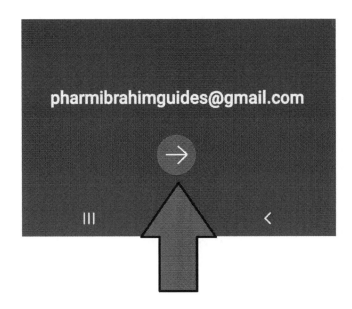

5. Read the terms and conditions by tapping the go icon next to each terms and conditions. If you agree to all the terms and conditions, tap **I have read and agreed to all of the above**. Then tap next icon . *If you don't agree to all terms/conditions, simply select the one you agree to and click the next icon* . Please note that you would need to agree to **Bixby Privacy Policy** to continue.

6. Follow the onscreen instructions to setup and register your voice so that Bixby can recognize your voice.

7. After the voice setup, you would see a screen like the one below.

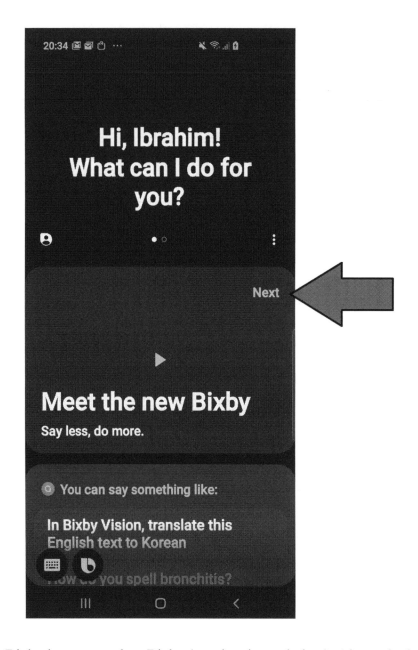

8. Tap Bixby icon to speak to Bixby (see the picture below). Alternatively, tap the keyboard icon to use a keyboard to ask your question. In addition, you can tap the menu icon located at the top of the screen to access options like **settings, quick commands, tutorials** and more.

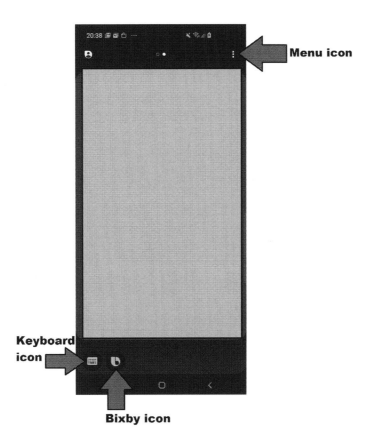

Bixby Home

Bixby Home allows you to access some specific information from your Home screen.

To access and use Bixby Home:

1. Swipe right while on the Home screen and tap **Continue**/**Start**. You might need to swipe more than once before you access Bixby Home.

2. Read the terms and conditions by tapping each terms and conditions. If you agree to all the terms and conditions, tap **I agree to all**, then tap **Next/Start**. *If you don't agree to all terms/conditions, simply select the one you agree to and click* **Next/Start**. Follow the prompts to complete the setup.

3. Bixby Home displays specific information in form of cards. To access a card, simply tap the card.

4. To refresh a card or pin a card to the top, tap the menu icon next to the card and select an appropriate option. See the picture below.

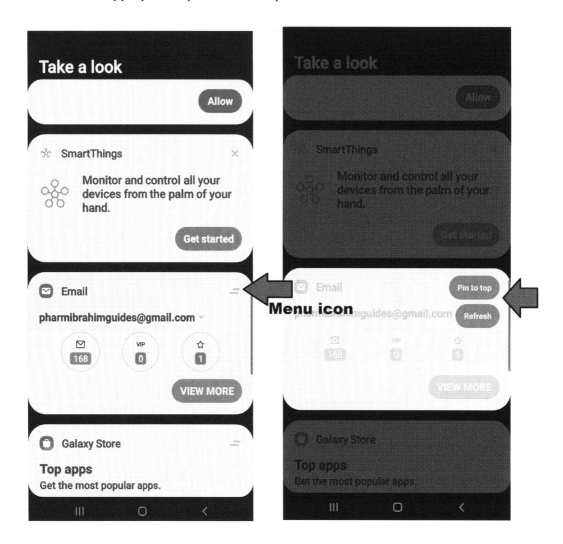

5. To adjust Bixby settings, tap the menu icon ⦙ located at top of the screen and tap **Settings**. Then choose an option.

Tip: To choose which card is displayed to you on the Bixby home page, tap the menu icon

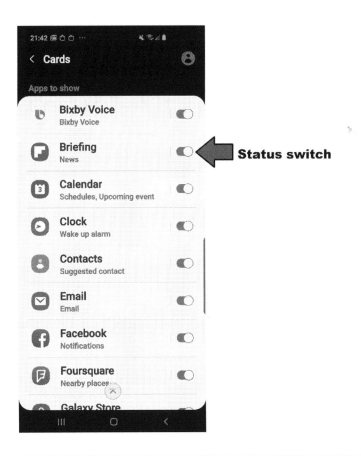 found at the top of the screen and tap **Cards.** Use the status switch to turn off/on a card. You can use this method to narrow the number of cards shown to you on the Bixby Home.

To customize the type of briefing you receive on the Bixby home page, tap the menu icon ⋮ located at the top of the screen and select **Cards**. Select **Briefing** and select the categories of news you want.

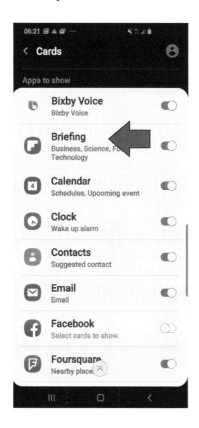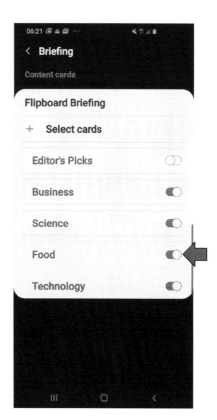

Bixby Voice

Bixby voice allows you to interact with Bixby using your voice.

Speaking to Bixby

One of the ways you would interact with Bixby is by speaking to it. The other way would be to use the keyboard icon .

To get Bixby into action, you would need to get its attention. To do that, perform any of the actions below:

1. Press the Bixby button located next to the volume button at the side of your phone and speak your command *while still pressing it*.

2. Alternatively, you can get Bixby's attention by saying **Hi Bixby!** However, you may need to enable this feature before you can put it to use. To enable **Hi Bixby** function:

   - Press the dedicated Bixby button once (the button located next to the volume button at the side of the phone).

   - Tap the menu icon located at top of the screen and select **Settings**.

   - Tap **Voice wake-up.** Make sure the indicator switch under **Wake with "Hi, Bixby"** is enabled (see the picture below).

   - If you want to increase the sensitivity of Bixby to the wake word, drag the slider under **Wake-up sensitivity** to medium or high position.

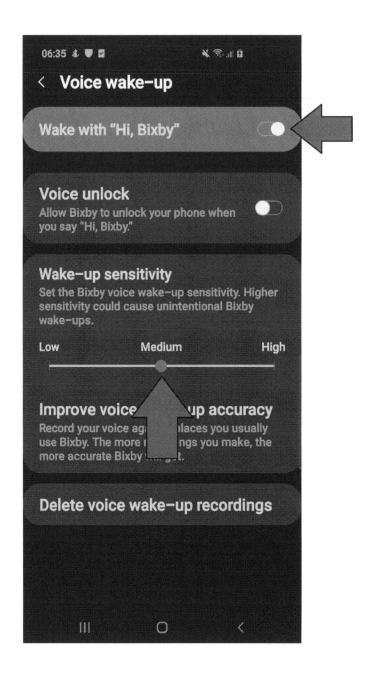

When Bixby is activated, it will respond by displaying an action box on the screen. Bixby will then give you an answer.

In addition, occasionally, you may notice that the question you asked Bixby is different from what it types into the action box. What Bixby types into the action box is what it thinks you have said.

Tip: You can train Bixby to recognize your voice better. To do this:

1. Press the dedicated Bixby button once (the button located next to the volume button at the side of the phone).

2. Tap the menu icon 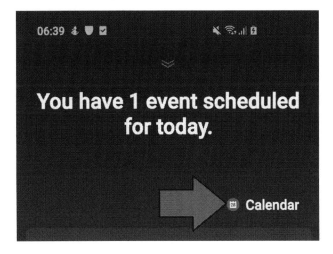 located at the top of the screen and tap **Settings**.
3. Tap **Voice wake-up**.
4. Tap **Improve voice wake-up accuracy** and follow the onscreen instructions.

In addition, you could change the voice of Bixby to a male voice. To do this, repeat steps 1 and 2 above and select **Language and voice style**. Then select **John**.

Tip: Usually, you could get example commands when you tap the app icon that appears after giving a command. For example, if you give a calendar-related command, you should see a small calendar app icon after you finish giving the command. Simply tap this icon to see more example commands.

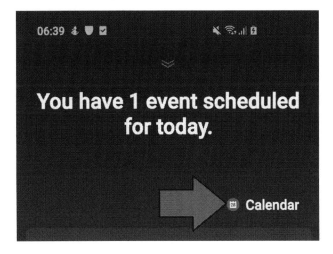

What about Typing?

The interesting thing is that Bixby can also listen when you command it using the on-screen keyboard. You can type in command and get a similar result just as you would get by speaking to it. This is a great feature especially if you can't speak to Bixby for one reason or the other e.g. if you are in a noisy place or your microphone is not working properly.

To use the Bixby typing feature:

1. Press the Bixby button once (located next to the volume button).

2. Tap the keyboard icon located at the bottom of the screen

3. Type your command.

4. Tap the send icon and wait for a reply. Alternatively, tap **Go** on the on-screen keyboard.

Using Quick Commands to Manage Bixby Like a Pro

Quick commands allow you to use Bixby in a special way. When you say a specific quick command, you trigger a set of actions from Bixby.

Quick Commands include:

a) Good morning b) I'm going out c) On my way d) I'm driving etc.

For example, if you say **Good Morning**, a set of actions (attached to Good Morning) are performed by Bixby.

To access quick command menu:

1. Press the dedicated Bixby button once (the button located next to the volume button at the side of the phone).

---

2. Tap the menu icon ⋮ located at top of the screen and tap **Quick commands**.

3. Then tap a quick command. Let's use **Good morning** quick command as an example.

    a) Tap **Daily Routine**.

    b) Select "Good Morning".

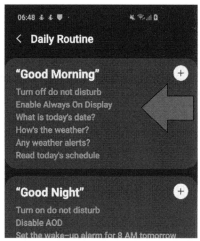

    b) Tap **Add a command** to add new command. Then tap on **Select a command**. Tap an app or a category. Then choose example commands from the list.

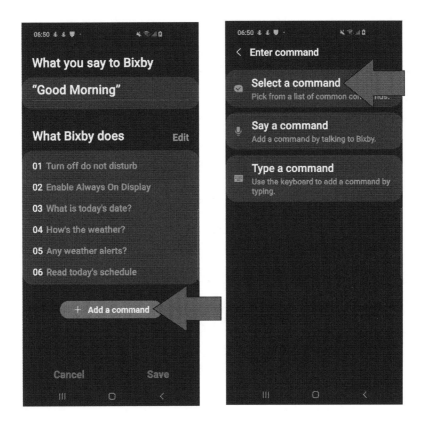

Alternatively, scroll down and select **Say it** or **Type it** to say or type your command.

c) To delete a command, tap **Edit** and select the **X** icon next to the command you want to delete. Tap **Done** to save the changes.

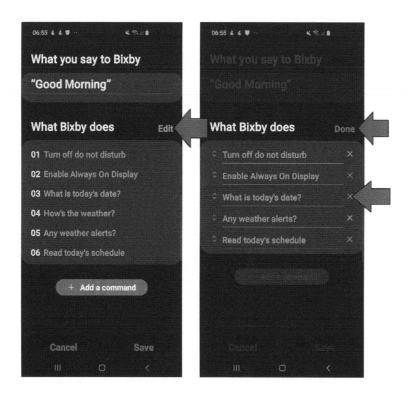

d) To change **Good Morning** to another phrase or statement, tap it and edit the name as you wish.

e) Tap **Save** to save the changes.

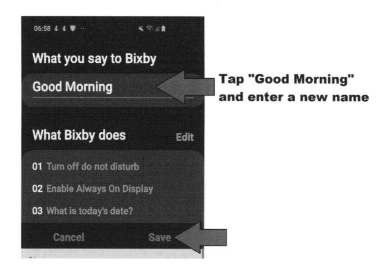

f) After tapping "Save", **Good Morning** should appear under **My commands** tab.

To access "My Commands" tab, tap on the back icon 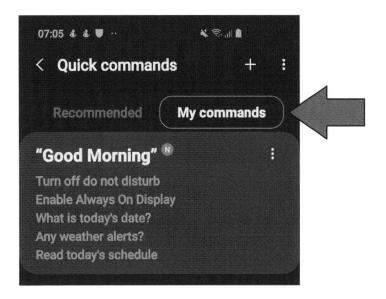 (if needed).

g) To delete a quick command, tap and hold it and select **Delete**.

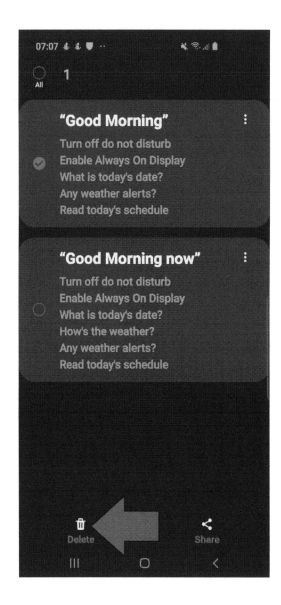

That is all! Now you can get Bixby to perform all the chosen commands by saying **Good Morning**.

Tip: You could add more quick commands by tapping the plus icon + located on the top of the screen. Then follow the prompts.

Using Bixby to Open Apps or Programs

One of those things you would probably want to use Bixby for is accessing your apps. You can quickly open an app by saying **Open**, then mention the name of the app. For example, to open settings, say or type **Open settings.** To open calculator, say **Open calculator**.

In addition, you may give a more specific command like **Open Wi-Fi Settings** to open the Wi-Fi settings. To turn off wireless network, say **Turn off wireless network** and so on.

Using Bixby with Notification

To access your notification, simply say **Do I have any notification?**

Using Bixby with Calendar

One of the fantastic things that Bixby can do for you is making an appointment. This personal assistant is built to work with your device Calendar making it easy for it to make appointments.

With just a few commands, you can get Bixby to put an event or appointment into your Calendar. **To do this:**

1. Press the Bixby button located next to the volume button at the side of your phone and say your command while still pressing it. Alternatively, say **Hi Bixby!**

2. Say whatever you want to include in the Calendar. For example, you can say any of the following:

   - Appointment with Clinton for Monday at 1 p.m.

   - Add meeting with Ibrahim at 10 a.m. on Sunday to my calendar.

   - Read today's schedule.

Please note that you can also say all the examples given above in other ways. The most important thing is to get Bixby to understand what you are saying.

To edit your events, go to the calendar app. After opening the calendar app, simply tap on the event you want to edit and make any necessary adjustment.

In addition, you can check how your calendar looks. To do this, click the microphone button and say, "**What is on my calendar today?**" or say, "**Any appointment today**?" or just any variant. Note that you can also ask Bixby about your calendar for a day in the future. To do this, say "**Any appointment schedule for tomorrow?**" or say, "**Any appointment on November 1st?**"

In addition, you could cancel an event by saying **Cancel tomorrow's event**. Or say **Cancel today's event.**

Tip: In case Bixby sets a wrong appointment, you can edit it in the calendar app using your on-screen keyboard instead of trying to say another word. Editing any mistake with keyboard appears smarter and faster.

In addition, instead of speaking, you may type the commands mentioned above into the search box to get a similar result.

Tip: You could get example commands by tapping on the calendar app icon (see the picture below) that usually appears after making a calendar related command.

Using Bixby to Set Reminders

There are probably many things going through your mind and it will be quite helpful if you can get a virtual assistant to remind you of some of your duties. Fortunately, Bixby can help you in this regard.

To set a reminder using Bixby:

1. Press the Bixby button located next to the volume button at the side of your phone and say your command while still pressing it. Alternatively, say **Hi Bixby!**

2. Say whatever you want to set a reminder for. For example, you can say the following:

   - Remind me to fix the car by 3 p.m.

- Remind me to drop the bread at the restaurant.

- Remind me to pick my daughter by 4 p.m.

- Remind me to call Ibrahim at 1 p.m. and so on.

Please note that it is probably not compulsory that you put **remind** in every statement as I did above. But I would advise that you to do so whenever you can. This is because it will help Bixby to easily get what you are saying and avoid any confusion.

Note: In case Bixby sets a wrong reminder, you can edit it in the Reminder app using your on-screen keyboard. In addition, to see all your reminders, simply say **Show me my reminders**. Or say **Show me my reminders for today**.

Tip: You could get example commands by tapping on reminder app icon (see the picture below) that usually appears after making a reminder-related command.

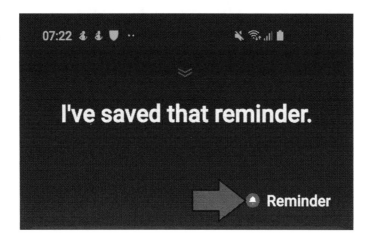

Using Bixby with Alarm and Timer

You can also set an alarm or timer using this virtual assistant.

To do this:

1. Repeat the first step mentioned above.

2. Say the time for alarm. For example, you can say: "**set an alarm for 1 p.m. every Monday**" or "**alarm for 1 p.m. every Wednesday**" or "**set an everyday alarm for 2 p.m.**" or "**set an alarm for 1 p.m. on 24th of October**".

3. To set a timer, you might say **Set a timer for 15 minutes**.

4. When it has grabbed the information, the alarm would appear and it will tell you that it has set the alarm.

5. To cancel an alarm, you might say **Cancel my alarm** or say **turn off all my alarms**.

You could get example commands by tapping on Alarm and Timer app icon (see the picture below) that usually appears after making an alarm or timer related command.

Using Bixby with Clock

You can ask Bixby what your local time is. In addition, it can also tell you the time in a specific place.

1. Say **Hi Bixby!**

2. Then say, "**What is the time?**" or say, "**What is the time in Seattle?**"

Using Bixby to Get Flight Information

You can also use this virtual assistant to get information about a flight. This is a smarter way to know when an airplane will take off.

For example, you can say **Status of Southwest flights from Los Angeles to San Francisco** to get the information about this flight.

You could get example commands by tapping on Flight app icon (see the picture below) that usually appears after making a flight related command.

Using Bixby with Weather App

To know about the weather condition of a place, just say "**What's the weather going to be like today?**". You may also know about the weather condition of a place by asking "**What is the weather condition of New York today?**"

Using Bixby with Mail App

You can instruct Bixby to compose an email for you. To do this:

1. Press the Bixby button located next to the volume button at the side of your phone and speak your command while still pressing it. Alternatively, say **Hi Bixby!**

2. Then give the command. For example, you can say:

- Send an email to Clinton.

- Send an email to Clinton and Steve.

- Search for emails from Pharm Ibrahim.

- Read me unread emails

- Show all the emails I received today.

- Show me my unread emails.

- Read all the emails marked as important.

- Search for emails from Steve and mark them as important.

Please note that you will usually have to include one or more information before you send the email. Simply follow the voice prompts to add subject and email body.

You could get example commands by tapping on the email app icon (see the picture below) that usually appears after making email related commands.

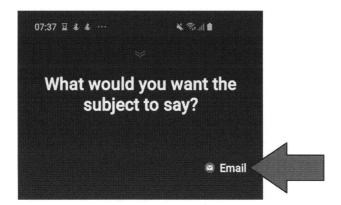

Using Bixby to Make a Phone Call

You can ask Bixby to make a call. For example, you can say "Hi Bixby" followed by:

- Call Pharm Ibrahim

- Block Steve's number

- Delete calls from Robert

- Do I have missed calls?

You could get example commands by tapping on the phone app icon (see the picture below) that usually appears after making call related commands.

Using Bixby with Map App

You can also use Bixby to search the map. This virtual assistant is built to work with the Map app on your device. **To get how the map of a place looks like**:

1. Press the Bixby button located next to the volume button at the side of your phone and speak your command while still pressing it. Alternatively, say **Hi Bixby!**

2. Then say the map of an area you want to get. For example, you may say:

   - Map of Seattle.

- Show me the map of Seattle.

What about Math?

Bixby can also help you with some mathematical calculations and conversions. For example, you can ask Bixby **What is the square root of four?** You can also say **convert one meter to centimeter** or **convert 1 ton to grams**.

Using Bixby to Get Definitions

Also, you can ask Bixby for meaning of words. For example, you may say **what is the meaning of flabbergasted?**

Bixby Voice Settings

The settings tab allows you to manage Bixby's functions. To access Bixby's settings:

1. Press the dedicated Bixby button once (the button located next to the volume button at the side of the phone).

2. Tap the menu icon ⋮ and tap **Settings**.

3. Tap an option.

The settings menu allows you to manage Bixby better. I would recommend that you take time to go through the various settings options on the settings page.

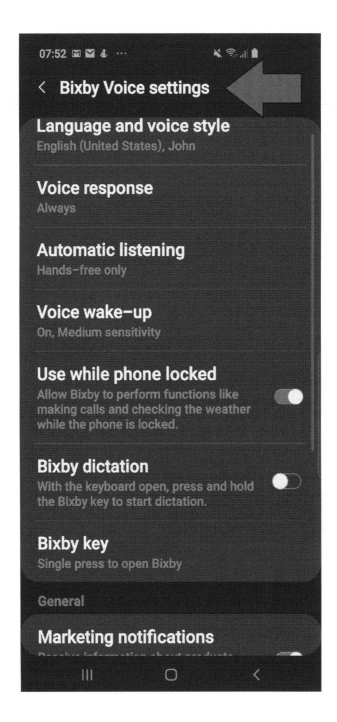

How to Control Your Privacy When Using Bixby Voice

To control how Bixby manages/accesses your information:

4. Press the dedicated Bixby button once (the button located next to the volume button at the side of the phone).

5. Tap the menu icon ⋮ located at the top/middle part of the screen and tap **Settings**.

6. Tap **Privacy.**

7. Tap an option to disable or enable.

Troubleshooting Bixby

Although much efforts have been put into making this virtual assistant, it is possible that Bixby misbehaves at one time or the other. When this happens, there are few things to do.

- **Ensure that you are connected to a strong network**: If you have a bad or no internet connection, Bixby may not work properly. Therefore, the first thing to check when Bixby starts to misbehave is the internet connection.

- **Use the Virtual Keyboard**: You may need to use the keyboard to pass your message to Bixby if you find out that it is not getting your speech. Many of what you say (if not all) can also be typed into the Bixby's search bar. Please go to page 178 to learn more about this.

- **Close the Bixby Voice app and press the Bixby button to access it again**.

- **Try to Restart Your Phone**: If you find out that the methods mentioned above do not work, try restarting your phone.

Conclusion

Bixby is like a learning machine and it is being improved upon. If you are having difficulty passing your message across to it, you may try typing (see page 178) some of your commands into the command box. I strongly believe you will know how to use it more as time goes on.

Bixby Vision

Bixby Vision allows you to interact with images in an educating manner. It also gives you more understanding of what you are looking at. When first using Bixby Vision, you may need to agree to some terms and conditions.

To Use Bixby Vision:

1. Launch the camera app of your phone.
2. Aim the lens of the camera at what you want to capture.
3. Tap the Bixby button. You can use the Bixby Vision to extract texts, translate a language, scan Barcodes etc. If you are using Bixby Vision for the first time, simply follow the on-screen instructions to set it up. Please note that you may need to agree to terms and conditions when setting up Bixby Vision. To do this, scroll down to read all the terms/conditions and agree as appropriate.

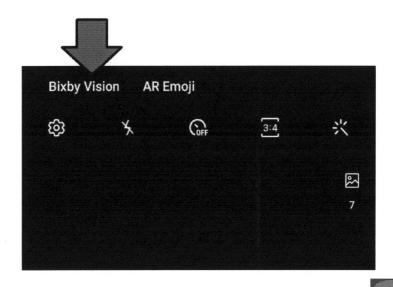

An alternate way to access Bixby Vision is tapping on Bixby Vision icon 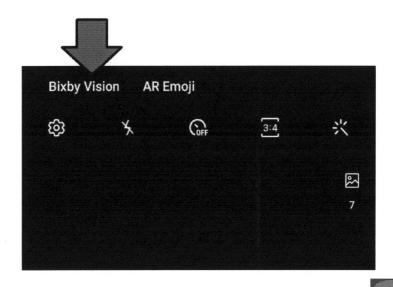 located on the applications screen.

4. Bixby vision would then automatically try to recognize what you are viewing. To extract out a text, select **Extract**.

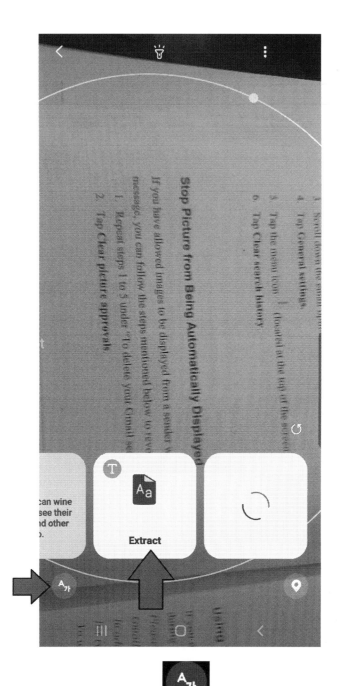

5. To translate, tap the translation button 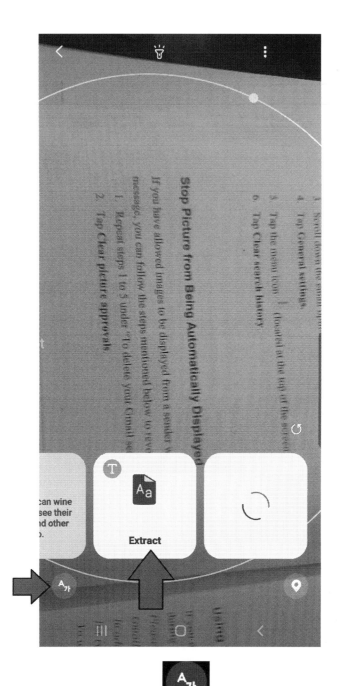 (see the picture above) and select the language you want to translate to. Then wait for Bixby to make the translation. After the translation is done, you would see **translated by Google** at the bottom of the screen. Tap 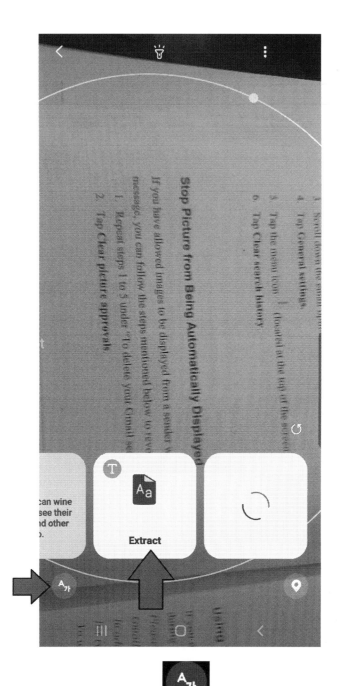 to open the translation in a new tab.

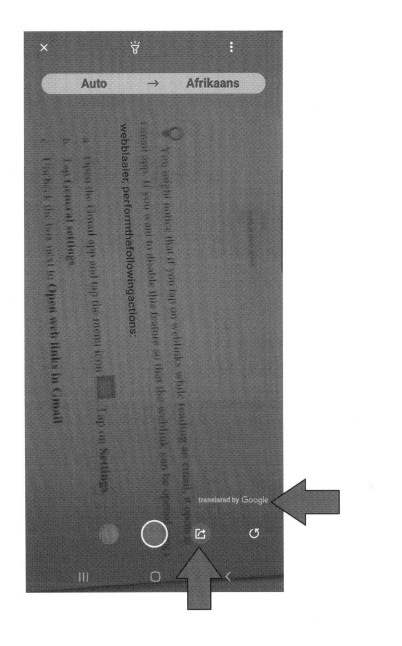

6. To manage Bixby Vision settings, tap the menu icon ⋮ (found at the top of the screen) and select **Settings**.

7. To exit, tap the back button ◀.

You can also access Bixby vision while using the Gallery app. Simply launch the **Gallery** app, tap an image and tap the Bixby button (found at the bottom of the screen). Please note that some pictures may not have a Bixby button.

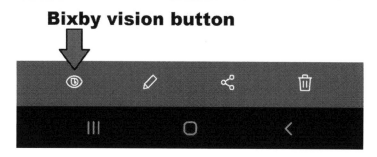

Tip: If Bixby vision is misbehaving, you can clear its data so that you start using it anew. To do this:

1. Swipe down from the top of the screen and select the settings icon .
2. Tap **Apps**.
3. Then tap on the **Bixby Vision** from the list of applications.
4. If you want to clear all your data on the Bixby Vision app and start using it like a new app, tap **Storage** and select **Clear data**.

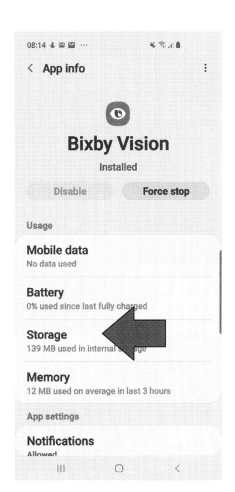

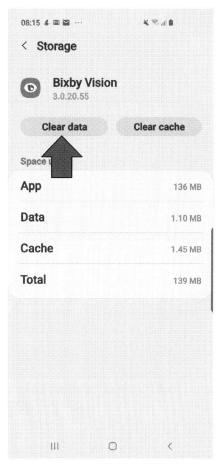

Using the Web

Internet App

Opening the Internet Browser

The first thing you would need to do to use the Internet app is to open it. To do this:

1. From the Home/App screen, tap **Internet** .

2. If you are using the Internet app for the first time, follow the prompts to get started.

Get to Know the Internet Browser Interface

When you open the Internet app, you should see the following buttons/icons:

Discover the Galaxy

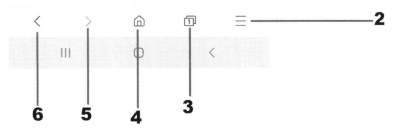

1	**Refresh:** Tapping this icon reloads a webpage.
2	**Menu icon:** Tap this icon to access additional options such as **Settings**, **Find on page**, **Print, Bookmarks** etc.

3	**Tabs:** Tap this to navigate between different webpages.
4	**Home:** Tap this icon to go to the browser's Home page.
5	**Forward**: Tap this icon to return to the page you just left.
6	**Back:** Tap this icon to revisit the page you just visited. To quickly access browsing history, tap and hold the back button $<$
7	**In-website menu icon**: You could access the tabs/menus in a website by tapping on this icon. Please note not all website has this button.
8	**Favorite**: Tap this icon to bookmark a webpage.

Customizing the Home Page

The Home page is the page that opens when you open your Internet browser app. Fortunately, you can choose what appears on your Internet Home page.

To do this:

- While the Internet browser is opened, tap the menu icon ≡ (found at the bottom of the screen), then tap on **Settings.**

- Tap **Home page** and choose an option.

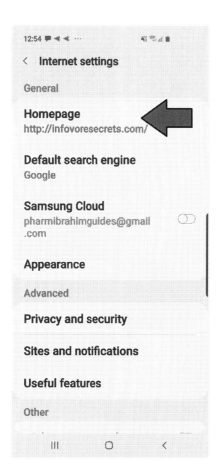 

- Tap the back button  to save the changes.
- To go to the Home page while using your internet browser, tap the internet browser Home button .

Using the Address/Search Bar

Every web browser must have an address bar and your Internet browser also has one. This bar serves the function of URL address bar and search bar. By default, the searches done on this bar is executed by Google. To learn how to change the search engine to another one, go to page 215.

You choose whether to launch a webpage or search for a term based on what you type into the address bar. For example, if you type **Infovore Secrets** into the address bar and tap **Go**, Google search results for that phrase is displayed. On the other hand, if you type **infovoresecrets.com** and tap **Go**, you will be taken to the website bearing the name.

Internet browser makes website suggestions to you based on the sites you have recently visited, to choose any of this suggested site, tap it.

When you begin to type inside the address bar, Internet browser automatically makes suggestions beneath your typing. You can choose any of these suggestions to make things faster.

Zooming a Webpage in Internet Browser

To zoom in a webpage in Internet browser, place two fingers on the webpage and spread them apart. To zoom out, place two fingers on the webpage and move them closer. To force zoom a webpage that doesn't readily respond to a zoom request, turn on the **Manual zoom.** To do this, while the Internet browser is opened, tap the menu icon ☰ located at the bottom of the screen, and then tap on **Settings**. Select **Appearance** and tap the status switch next to **Control the zoom on webpages** to enable it.

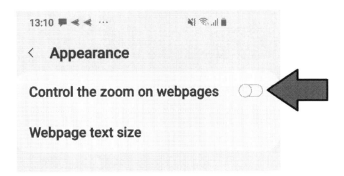

Using Tabs on Internet Browser

The tabs allow you to open different webpages at once. You can open many tabs at once in the Internet browser.

To manage browsing tabs:

1. Tap the tab icon 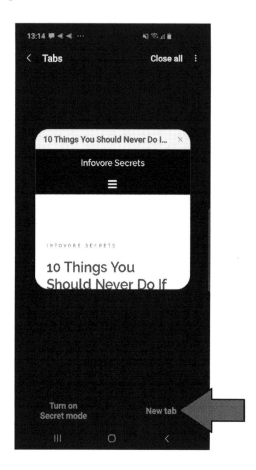 located at the bottom of the screen.
2. To open a new tab, tap **New Tab**.

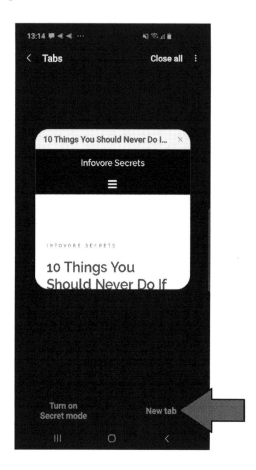

3. To access a tab you have opened before, tap the tab icon 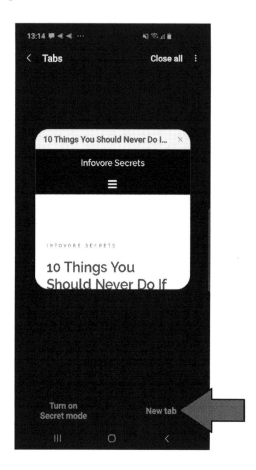 and tap your desired tab.
4. To close a tab, tap the **X** icon at the top right corner of the thumbnail of the tab you want to close.
5. To close all tabs, while on the tabs' screen, tap **Close All** located at the top of the screen.

Tip: You can quickly move from one tab to another. To do this, simply swipe left/right on the address bar.

Favorites (Bookmarks)

With several billions of webpages on the internet, you just have to select your favorites. Just like other modern day browsers, your Samsung Galaxy device Internet browser gives you the opportunity to select a favorite or bookmark a page. This makes it easier to visit the website or webpage in the future.

To bookmark a webpage:

1. Open the website you want to bookmark.

2. Tap the menu icon ≡ found at the bottom of the screen and select **Add page to**.

3. Select **Bookmarks** from the list.

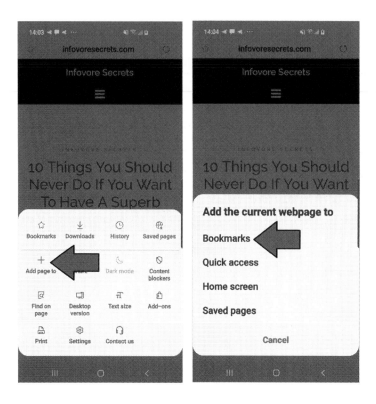

4. Key in the **Title** you want.

5. Tap **Save.**

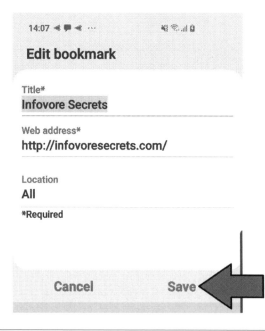

6. By default, your bookmarks would be stored under **All** folder. To save a bookmark in a new folder:

    a) Repeat steps 1 to 3 above.

    b) Tap **All**, then tap **Create folder**.

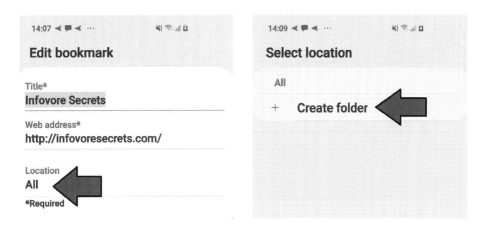

    c) Enter a name and tap **Create**.

    d) Then tap this newly created folder and then tap **Select**.

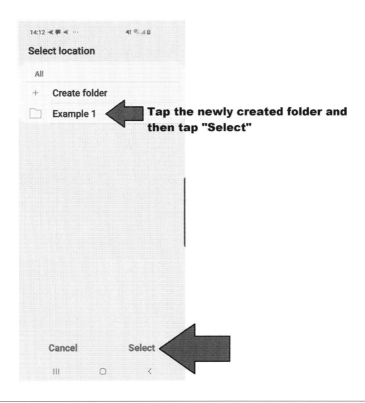

e) Thereafter, enter a name for your bookmark and tap **Save.**

Tip: To quickly add a bookmark, just open the webpage and tap favorite icon  next to the address bar.

Accessing Your Bookmarks/Favorites

After you have added a webpage to your favorite list, you would need to access this list sooner or later. To access your bookmarks, tap the menu icon ☰, and select **Bookmarks**.

Saving a Webpage

Webpages contain a lot of information and you would probably need to schedule some webpages for later reading. Saving a webpage is a great way to do this. When you find an interesting information online and you don't have the time to read it, you can save it for later reading.

To save a webpage, open the webpage and tap menu icon ≡. Then select **Add page to** and then select **Saved pages**.

Accessing Your Saved Pages

After you have saved a page, you would need to access this page sooner or later. To do this, tap the menu icon (see the picture below) and tap **Saved Pages**.

To delete a saved page, tap and hold the page you want to delete and select **Delete**.

Changing the Search Engine

The default search engine on your Internet browser is Google. Some people may love to change this to another search engine.

You can change the Internet browser Search Engine by following the steps highlighted below:

1. While the browser is opened, tap the menu icon ☰ (found at the bottom of the screen) and select **Settings**.

2. Tap on **Default search engine** and select a search engine.

Making Internet App Your Default Browser

If you have multiple browsers on your device, you can make Internet app your default browser. To do this:

1. Swipe down from the top of the screen and select the settings icon .

2. Tap **Apps** and tap the menu icon ⋮ .

3. Tap **Default apps**.

4. Tap **Browser app** and choose **Samsung Internet**.

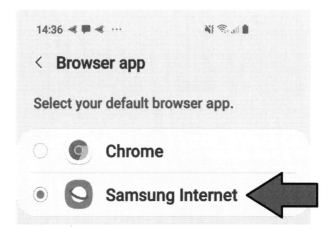

Tip: You can use the method mentioned above to set other favorite app(s) as default app(s). For example, if you have many messaging apps on your device, you can select a default messaging app using this method.

Managing the History List

If the secret mode is not enabled, your Internet browser collects the history of the webpages you visit and stores them.

To access your history:

1. Tap the menu icon ≡ (located at the bottom of the screen).

2. Tap **History**.

Tip: To clear the browsing data, tap the menu icon ≡ (found at the bottom of the screen) > **Settings** > **Privacy and security** > **Delete browsing data**. Select what you would like to delete and tap **Delete.**

In addition, if you see that a website/webpage is misbehaving, you can try deleting the *cache, cookies and site data* and see if this would solve the problem. Tap the menu icon ≡ (found at the bottom of the screen) > **Settings** > **Privacy and security** > **Delete browsing data**. Select **Cache, Cookies and site data** and tap **Delete**.

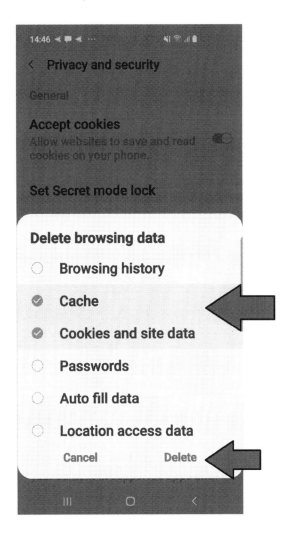

Sharing a Webpage with Friends

To share a webpage with friends, open the Internet app and tap the menu icon ☰ found at the bottom of the screen. Tap on **Share**. Then choose an app and follow the prompts.

Add Your Favorite Webpage to the Home Screen

You can make your favorite webpage a shortcut on the Home screen. This allows you to easily access the webpage directly from your Home screen. To do this:

1. Open a webpage and tap on the menu icon ☰ (found at the bottom of the screen).

2. Tap **Add page to**.

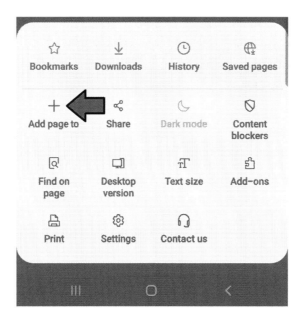

3. Tap **Home screen**.

4. Tap **Add**.

5. To see the newly added webpage, tap the home button ⬭ (located at the bottom of the screen). If you can't see it on the first Home screen, swipe left to check another Home screen.

Printing Web Pages on the Internet browser

Printing on the Internet browser is quite fantastic. You can initiate the printing process by tapping on the menu icon ☰ (found at the bottom of the screen). Then tap **Print.** Tap the **dropdown arrow** to select a printer and follow the prompts (see the picture below). To adjust the printing options, tap **Copies**.

To save the webpage as a pdf, tap the dropdown arrow and select **Save as PDF.**

Thereafter, tap the yellow **PDF** icon 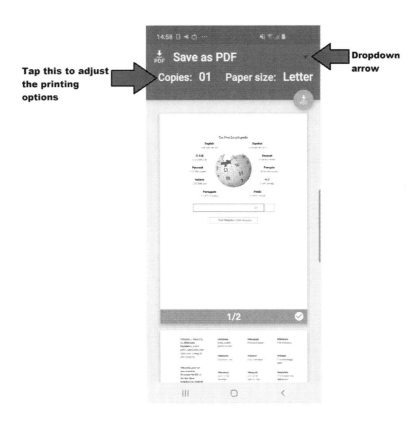 and choose a folder. Then tap **Done** to download.

To locate the file you just downloaded, from the applications screen, go to **Samsung** folder > **My Files** > **Internal storage**. Then tap on the folder where you stored the downloaded file. If needed, tap the downloaded PDF file to open it.

Secret Mode

There are times when you will not want your browser to save any information about your visit to a webpage. For instance, if you don't want a website to save cookies on your device or you don't want your children to know you are browsing about favorite gifts to buy for them.

In addition, secret mode browsing allows for (multiple) concurrent access of a single site. For example, you may access your Yahoo mail account (or another web account) on a normal window and use the secret mode tab to open the Yahoo mail account of that of your friend or family member without logging out of your account. Pages viewed in secret mode are not listed in your browser history or search history and leave no traces (such as cookies) on your device.

To activate the Secret mode, in the toolbar at the bottom of the screen, tap the tabs icon

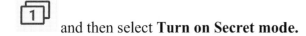 and then select **Turn on Secret mode.**

Then tap **Set password** to protect your secret mode data with a password. You may also tap **Don't use password** if you don't want to use a password.

To deactivate the Secret mode, close the Internet app. Alternatively, tap the tab button

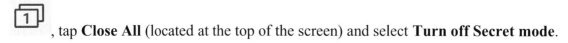, tap **Close All** (located at the top of the screen) and select **Turn off Secret mode**.

Samsung Pass

Samsung Pass allows you to easily log in into websites by storing login information for you. You would need to set up biometrics to use Samsung Pass. You can use Samsung Pass to autofill your username and password.

To use Samsung Pass:

1. Swipe down from the top of the screen and tap the **settings icon** .

2. Tap **Biometrics and Security**.

3. Scroll down and tap **Samsung Pass**.

4. Carefully follow the on-screen information to set up this feature.

5. After the setup, you can click on **Autofill forms** and add your shipping address and card information. This would allow you to quickly use this information to fill forms in the future.

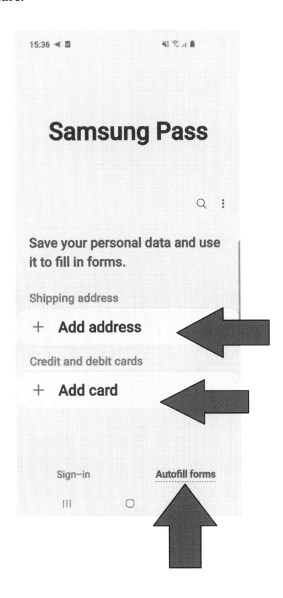

Thereafter, make sure the autofill option is set to use Samsung Pass. To do this:

1. Swipe down from the top of the screen and tap the settings icon .

2. Tap the search bar located at the top of the screen and type in **Autofill** into the search bar. The result filters as you type. In the search result, select **Autofill service**. Then tap **Autofill service** again and make sure that **Autofill with Samsung Pass** is selected.

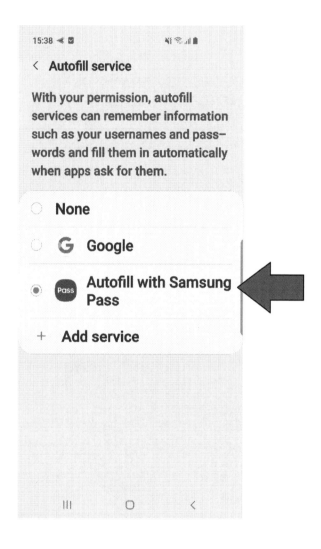

That is all. The next time you sign in to a website or service in Samsung Internet or sign in to an app, you should be prompted to save your username and password in Samsung Pass. Simply select **Remember/Save** when prompted.

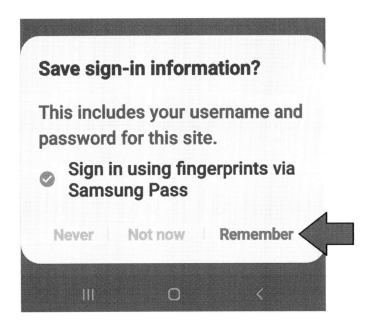

More on the Menu Icon

Many options under the **menu** tab ☰ (found at the bottom of the screen) have already been discussed, but I would still like to point out a few more things.

1. **Find on page:** Use this option to search for a word or a phrase on a webpage.

2. **Desktop version:** Use this option to request the desktop version of a webpage.

3. **Dark mode:** Use this option to give a webpage a darkish background.

4. **Add-ons:** This allows you to do more when using the Internet app. To see which add-ons are available on your Internet app, tap **Add-ons**.

5. **Contents blockers**: Tap this option to access apps that block ads.

Troubleshooting the Internet browser

The Internet browser may sometimes refuse to work properly, or it may hang. If this happens, just close the browser and open it again. To close the Internet app, tap the recent button 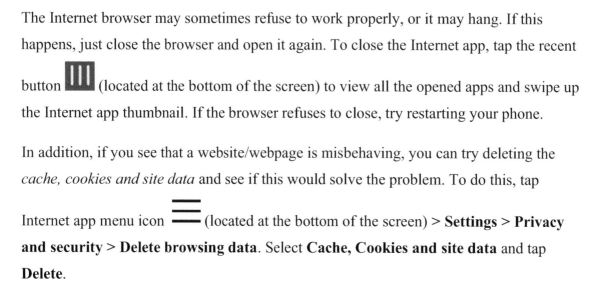 (located at the bottom of the screen) to view all the opened apps and swipe up the Internet app thumbnail. If the browser refuses to close, try restarting your phone.

In addition, if you see that a website/webpage is misbehaving, you can try deleting the *cache, cookies and site data* and see if this would solve the problem. To do this, tap Internet app menu icon ═ (located at the bottom of the screen) > **Settings** > **Privacy and security** > **Delete browsing data**. Select **Cache, Cookies and site data** and tap **Delete**.

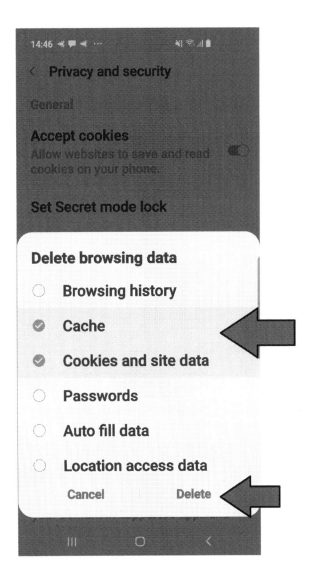

Troubleshooting Internet Connection when Using the Internet Browser

Internet browser may sometimes refuse to browse the internet. When this happens, you may try any of the suggestions below:

1. Check if you are connected to a wireless network. When Wi-Fi is connected, active and it is communicating with a wireless Access Point, **Wi-Fi active icon** is displayed on the status bar at the top of the screen. If your phone is not connected

to a network, swipe down from the top of the screen and tap the settings icon

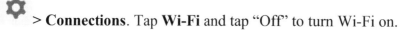 > **Connections**. Tap **Wi-Fi** and tap "Off" to turn Wi-Fi on.

2. If you are trying to use a cellular connection and not a Wi-Fi connection, then check your cellular data connection. Swipe down from the top of the screen, tap the settings icon ⚙ > **Connections** > **Data Usage**. Then make sure the switch next to **Mobile data** is turned on.

3. If you are trying to roam while abroad, check that you have allowed roaming. Swipe down from the top of the screen and tap the **settings icon** ⚙ > **Connections** > **Mobile networks** > **Data Roaming**. Then make sure the switch next to **Data Roaming** is switched on. Please note that when roaming, international roaming charges may apply.

If you can't still browse after trying all the options above, then make sure that you have not mistakenly/knowingly installed a new browsing setting on your phone. If you have installed new settings from a text message, then uninstall the new settings. To do this, swipe down from the top of the screen and tap the settings icon ⚙ > **Apps**. Look for the new settings. Tap the new settings and select **Uninstall**.

If you can't still browse after trying the suggestions above, I would recommend you contact your Internet service provider.

Communication

Calling

Learn how to use the calling functions, such as making and answering calls, using options available during a call and using call-related features.

Making, Answering, Rejecting and Silencing a Call

To make a call or silence a call:

1. While on the Home/App screen, tap **Phone** and enter a phone number. If the keypad does not appear on the screen, tap the **keypad** to show the keypad. To call a number on your contact, tap the **Contact** button on the Phone app screen.

2. To make a call from the **Recents** tab, tap the **Recents** tab located at the bottom of the screen.

3. To make a phone call, tap a contact and tap the phone icon .

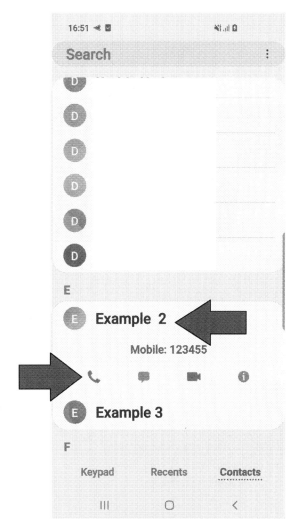

4. To silence the ring of an incoming call, press the volume button (located at the side of the phone).

Tip: You can access apps/items on your phone while receiving a call. To do this, tap the

Home key located at the lower side of the screen and tap the item/app you want to access.

To answer a call or reject an incoming call:

1. To receive an incoming call, tap or drag the green phone icon 📞 .

2. To decline an incoming call, tap or drag the red phone icon 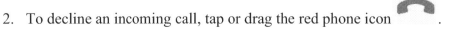 .

3. To reply with a text, swipe up from the bottom of the screen or tap **Send Message**.

4. Then tap one of the pre-written messages. Alternatively, tap **Compose new message** and type your message.

Tip: If you are using an app, a pop-up screen is displayed for the incoming call, just tap the corresponding icon to accept, decline the call or reply with a message.

In addition, you can create rejection messages of your own. From the Home/App screen,

tap **Phone** > **Menu icon** ⋮ > **Settings** > **Quick decline messages**, enter a message and tap plus icon **+.** To delete a message, tap the minus icon next to it.

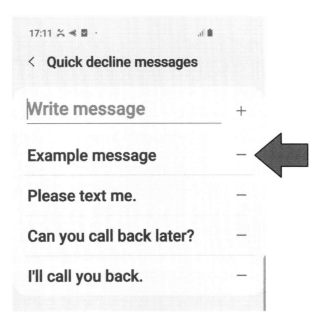

If a phone number calls you or you call a number and you don't have it on your contact list, you can easily add it to your contact list. To do this, tap **Phone** app and tap **Recents.** Then tap the contact and tap + **Add to Contacts** and follow the prompts.

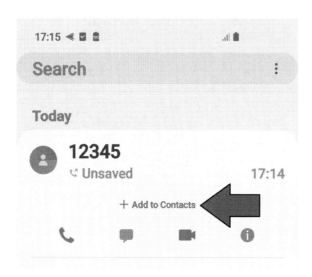

Changing the Ringing Tone

If you don't like the default ringtone, you could change it to another one. To do this:

1. Swipe down from the top of the screen and select settings icon 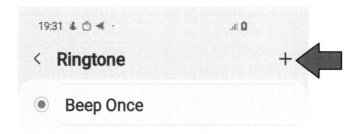. Tap **Sounds and Vibration** tab.
2. Tap **Ringtone**.
3. If needed, select a SIM.
4. If you don't what any sound, scroll up (if needed) and select **Silent**. Alternatively, if you want a very simple sound, select Beep Once.
5. To add your own alert type, tap the plus icon located at the top of the screen and follow the prompts.

6. To ensure that your phone ring out when you have a call, select **Sound mode** and choose **Sound**. If you don't want your phone to make any sound, select **Mute**.

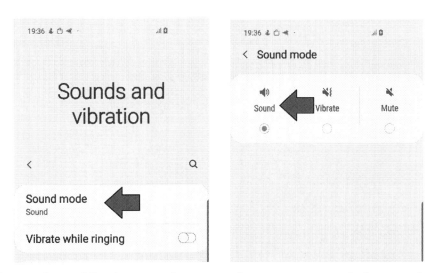

Tip: To change the notification sound on your phone, repeat step 1 above and tap **Notification sounds**. Select a SIM (if needed) and choose an appropriate sound.

Learn How to Use Your Phone During a Call

You can perform any of these tasks when on a call:

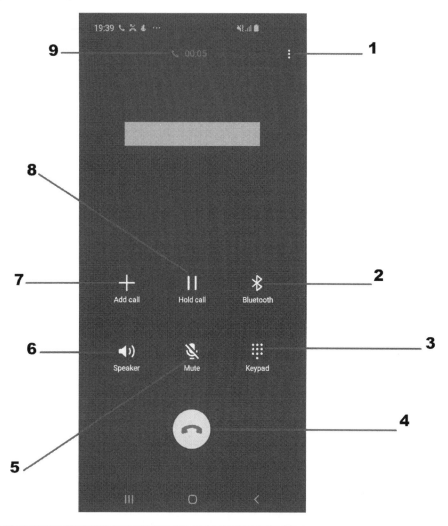

Number	Function
1.	Tap the **Menu icon** to view/add a contact or send a message.
2.	Tap the Bluetooth icon to connect to a Bluetooth device/headset while on a call.
3.	Tap the keypad icon to access the keypad. To hide the keypad, tap the **Hide** icon ▦.
4.	Tap the red phone icon to **end a call**.

5.	Tap this icon to mute the microphone.
6.	To turn speaker on or off, tap the speaker icon.
7.	Tap the plus icon to add another contact to a call or start another call.
8.	To hold the current call, tap **Hold call**
9.	Call time

Tip: To access the application screen while on a call, tap the Home button. If you want to return to the call screen, swipe down from the top of the screen and tap the current call.

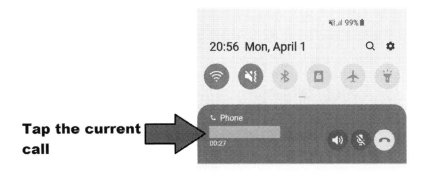

Place a New Call While on a Call (Conference Calling)

If your network service provider supports this feature, you can make another call while a call is in progress.

1. From the active call screen, tap + **Add call**.

2. Enter the new number and tap ![phone icon] **Dial**. When the call is answered:

    i.   Tap ![swap icon] **Swap** to switch between the two calls.

    ii.   Tap ![merge icon] **Merge** to turn the calls to a conference call.

3. To end a call while on a conference call, tap the dropdown arrow ![⌄] (next to **Conference call**) and select **Drop** next to the call you want to end.

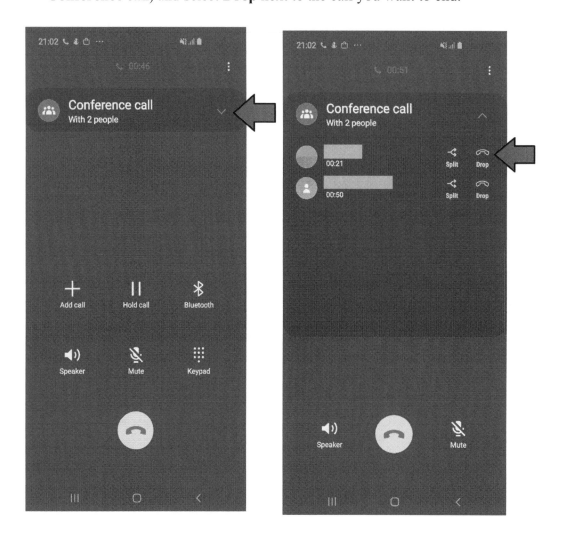

Emergency Calling

You can use Samsung Galaxy S10, S10 Plus and S10e to make an emergency call. From the Home screen, tap **Phone** icon and enter the emergency telephone number. Note that if you dial 911 in the U.S, your location details may be provided to an emergency service provider even if your settings does not support this.

Please note that an emergency number can be dialed even if the phone is locked.

Using Call Waiting

Call waiting allows you to get another call while you're already in one.

1. To answer the new call, tap or drag **Answer** to the right direction and choose an option:

   i.   **Put ...on hold** to place the previous caller on hold while you answer the new call.

   ii.   **End call with...** to end the previous call and answer the new call.

2. Once the other call is answered, tap the swap icon next to the contact or phone number you wish to continue talking to. The other(s) would be put on hold. To merge the calls, tap the merge icon.

Please note that call waiting may be disabled by default. To enable this feature, tap **Phone > Menu icon > Settings > Supplementary services** and tap the switch next to **Call waiting**.

Using the Speed Dial Options

The speed dial allows you to quickly access a number on your contact list. To set up a speed dial:

1. Tap the phone icon.
2. Tap **Contacts** located at the bottom of the screen.
3. Tap **menu icon** located at the top of the screen.
4. Tap **Speed dial numbers**.
5. To add a contact to the speed dial, tap the contact icon.

6. To change the speed dial number, tap the dropdown arrow and pick a number. Number one is reserved for voicemail.

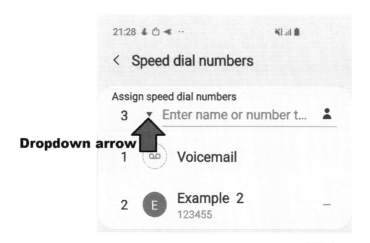

7. To call a contact you have added, tap the phone app icon and from the dial pad, press and hold the number assigned to the desired contact. To call a contact assigned to a two-digit speed dial, dial the first number, then press and hold the second number.

8. To delete a speed dial number, tap the **Minus (-)** icon next to the assigned contact. Removing a contact from a speed dial list will not delete it from your phone.

Using the Fixed Dialing Option

If you want to select the numbers your mobile phone can call, you need to turn on the fixed dialing. Once done, you can only call the selected numbers and emergency numbers.

1. From the Home screen, tap **Phone app icon** 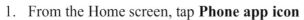 .

2. Tap **menu icon** located at the top of the screen.

3. Tap **Settings**.

4. Scroll down and tap **Supplementary services**.

5. Tap **Fixed dialing numbers**.

6. To turn the fixed dialing on, tap **Turn on FDN**, type in your **PIN2** and tap **OK**. Please contact your local network service provider for your PIN2.

7. To turn the fixed dialing off, tap **Turn off FDN**, enter your **PIN2** and tap **OK**.

Tip: I am not sure if all network providers support this feature. If you notice that this feature is not available on your phone or it is not working properly, you may need to contact your service provider to know if you can use this feature.

Adding Fixed Dialing Numbers

1. Repeat steps 1 to 5 above.

2. Tap **FDN List**.

3. Tap the menu icon ⋮ located at the top of the screen and select **Add**.

4. Tap **Name** and enter the required name.

5. Tap **Number** and enter the required phone number.

6. Tap **PIN2** and enter the PIN2. Please contact your local network service provider for your PIN2.

7. To import contacts, tap the menu icon ⋮ and select **Import from contacts**.

8. Tap the menu icon ⋮ again and select **SAVE** located at the top of the screen.

Please note that when FDN is enabled, you may not be able to call any other numbers apart from the numbers on the FDN list and the emergency numbers.

Call Forwarding (Diverting Calls to Another Number)

When you are busy, you can forward incoming calls to another phone number. Please note that your network provider would need to support this feature for it to be available.

1. From the Home screen, tap **Phone app icon** .

2. Tap **menu icon** located at the top of the screen.

3. Tap **Settings**.

4. Scroll down and tap **Supplementary services**.

5. Tap **Call forwarding**.

6. Select **Voice call** or **Video call**.

7. Tap the required divert type and follow the on-screen instructions. For example, to forward all your calls, tap **Always forward**.

8. To turn off call forwarding, select a divert type and select **turn off.**

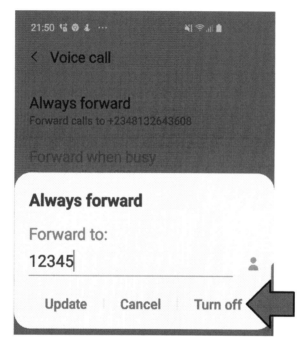

Tip: When the call forwarding option is enabled, you should see the call forwarding icon (see the picture below) on the notification bar at the top of the screen.

In addition, depending on your network provider, you may be able to forward calls to your voicemail and listen to them later. To know how to do this, contact your network service provider.

Block Calls

If your service provider supports this feature, you may be able to avoid receiving calls from certain numbers. Please note that the call blocking feature may not affect phone calls made or received via apps (e.g. Skype) installed on your device.

Please note that features available under Call blocking may differ from one service provider to another.

To block calls:

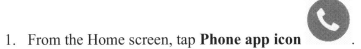

1. From the Home screen, tap **Phone app icon** .

2. Tap **menu icon** located at the top of the screen.

3. Tap **Settings**.

4. Tap **Block numbers**.

5. To add a number to your block list, enter the desired phone number in the **Add phone number** field, then tap the + icon. To add a number from your contacts, tap **Contacts** and then tap **Done** after adding the contact.

6. To remove a number from your block list, tap the Minus (-) icon next to a name or number on your block list.

7. To make sure that only the numbers that you have their contacts can call you, tap the status switch next to **Block unknown callers**.

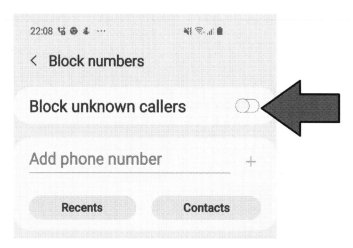

Tip: In certain instances, blocking anonymous call may be unbeneficial and even dangerous. For example, blocking anonymous calls may prevent you from accepting calls from those who have something important to tell you (unless you have their contacts).

In addition, if you are not able to use call blocking option after following the instructions above, please contact your network service provider.

Tip: To block a number from the call log, follow these steps:

1. From the Home screen, tap **Phone app icon** .

2. Tap **Recents** (located at the bottom of the screen).

3. Tap the number that you want to block and then tap details icon .

4. Tap **Block** located at the bottom of the screen.

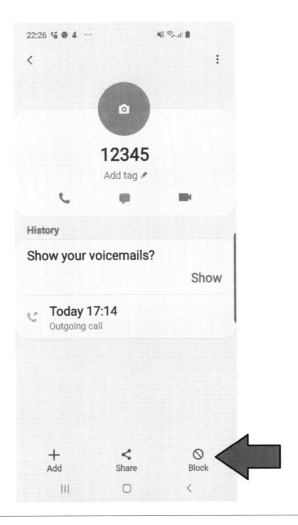

5. If you have the number you want to block on your contact list, while in Contact app, tap the contact you want to block. Tap the details icon (if needed). Tap menu icon 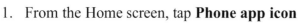 located at the top of the screen and then select **Block contact**.

What about Caller ID?

If your service provider supports this feature, you may prevent your service provider from displaying your number (ID) when you call another person.

1. From the Home screen, tap **Phone app icon** .

2. Tap **menu icon** located at the top of the screen.
3. Tap **Settings**.
4. Scroll down and tap **Supplementary services**.

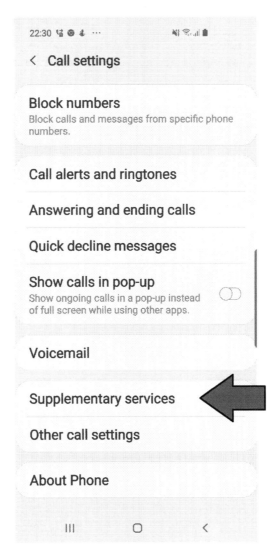

5. Tap **Show my caller ID** and choose an option.

Voicemail

Setting Up Voicemail

1. From the home screen, tap **Phone app icon** 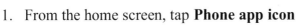 .

2. Tap the **Keypad** icon (found at the bottom of the screen) if needed.

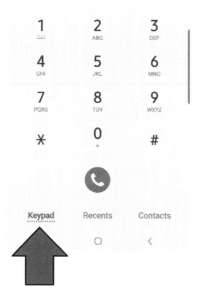

3. Press and hold **1** (on the virtual keyboard) and follow the prompts.

Please note that you might need to contact your network service provider to successfully set up a voicemail. For example, you might need to contact your network service provider to get a voicemail number or create a voicemail password.

Listening to Voicemail or Call Your Voicemail

1. To listen to your voicemail, open the Phone app.
2. Tap the **Keypad** icon found at the bottom of the screen (if needed).
3. Tap and hold number "1" (on the virtual keyboard) and follow the audio instructions to listen to your voicemails.

If the instructions above do not work for you, please contact your network service provider to know how to listen to and manage your voicemails.

Managing Voicemail settings

1. From the home screen, tap **Phone app icon** .

2. Tap **menu icon** located at the top of the screen.
3. Tap **Settings**.

4. If needed, scroll down and tap **Voicemail**.

5. Tap a setting to manage.

Tip: If your network provider supports it, you might be able to forward your unanswered calls to voicemail. To learn how to manage call forwarding options, see page 239-241. Please contact your network service provider to know how to forward calls to voicemail.

Using the Messaging app

This app allows you to send texts, images and video messages to other SMS and MMS devices.

To start or manage a conversation:

1. Tap the **Messages** app icon on the Home screen.

2. Tap the new message icon located at the bottom right corner of the screen.

3. Type in the first letters of the recipient's name. The list filters as you type. Then tap the required contact. Note; depending on your service provider, you can add up to 20 contacts (if not more). If you don't have the number on your contact, just key in the number in **Recipient** field (located at the top of the screen). To remove a contact from the send list, tap the minus icon (-) next to the contact.

   To access your contacts, tap the contact icon .

4. Tap the **Enter message** field and write the text for your SMS/MMS.

5. To attach a file such as audio, tap the plus icon and tap the menu icon ⋮ (if needed). Then choose an option.

6. When you are done, tap the send icon 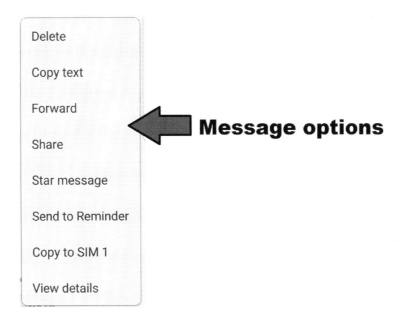. If prompted, tap **Send**.

7. To reply a message, tap the message and enter a message in the reply field. Tap the send icon when you are done.

8. To **Delete** a conversation, press and hold the message in question and tap on **Delete**. Then select **Delete** again (found at the bottom of the screen).

9. In a conversation, you can press and hold a message to **forward, copy, share** or **delete** the message.

Delete

Copy text

Forward ⬅ **Message options**

Share

Star message

Send to Reminder

Copy to SIM 1

View details

Tips:

- If you receive an attachment, you can tap on the attachment to view it. To save an attachment, tap and hold the attachment and select **Save attachment**. You can also tap the **Share** icon to share the attachment or **Delete** to delete an attachment. To view saved attachments, go to the app screen, tap **Samsung** folder, tap **My files** and tap a content category. Alternatively, visit **Photos/Gallery** app if the attachment is an image.

- To customize your message settings, open the Message app, tap the menu icon (found at the top of the screen) and select **Settings.** Tap the desired setting to adjust. To access more settings, tap **More Settings.** *Please note that the features available on message settings may differ from one service provider to another.*

- **You can block text messages** from certain numbers if your service provider supports this feature. To do this, open the Message app, and tap the menu icon

  > **Settings** > **Block numbers and messages** > **Block numbers**. Then enter the desired number in the **Enter number** field and tap the + icon to add the number to the block list. To select a number from your contacts/ message inbox, tap **Contacts/Inbox**. To remove a number from the message block list, tap the minus (-) icon.

- When you receive a message, you can easily save the number if it is not yet saved in your contacts. To do this, tap the Messaging app. Tap the conversation/message in question. Thereafter, tap **Add to Contacts** (located at the top of the screen). Follow the on-screen instructions to finish the process.

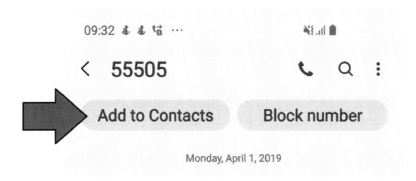

EMAIL APP

Introduction

Samsung Galaxy S10, S10 Plus and S10e come preloaded with an email app for sending and receiving emails. One of the things you would need to do when you start using this device is to set up an email account. In this section of the guide, I would be discussing how to use your Email app like a maven.

How to Add Your Email Accounts to the Email app

You probably have many email accounts and you may wish to add these accounts to the Email app on your device.

The email accounts you can add to the Email app include Google Mail and Yahoo Mail among others.

To add an email account:

1. Swipe down from the top of the screen and select settings icon .

2. Tap **Accounts and backup**.

3. Tap **Account.**

4. Tap **Add account.**

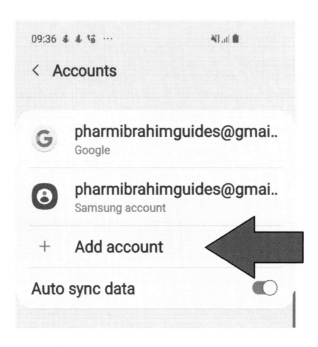

5. Tap **Email** and follow the prompts.

6. To add another email account, repeats steps 1 to 5 above.

Tip: If you are adding an Exchange account, repeat steps 1 to 4 above, select **Exchange** and follow the prompts. In addition, to add a Google account, repeat steps 1 to 4 above, tap **Google** and follow the prompts.

Special Note on Adding Exchange Account to the Email App

Following the instructions above might not be enough when you want to add your Exchange account to the Email app and you may need extra information. You may need to obtain from your Exchange administrator or provider the account's server address, domain name (and/or username) in addition to your email address and password.

How to Compose and Send an Email Message Using the Email App

You can easily send an email message to your friends or business colleagues using the Email App. In this section, we would be exploring how to compose and send an email message.

To send an email message:

- From the Home screen, swipe up and tap **Email** ![envelope icon]. If you can't see the Email app, check **Samsung** folder on the application screen and select **Email**.

- If you are using the Email app for the first time, follow the prompts to get started.

- To change to another email account if multiple email accounts are configured, swipe right from the left edge of the screen and tap an account.

- To compose a new email, tap the new email icon ![compose icon] located at the bottom of the screen.

- Tap the field next to **To** and type in the email address of the recipient. You can also tap the contact icon ![contact icon] to view and add contacts.

- To send a copy to another person, tap the dropdown icon ⌄ next to **To** and type the person's email address in the **Cc/Bcc** field.

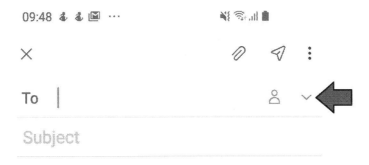

Tip: Cc means Carbon Copy. If you use the Cc option to send a message to many recipients, all the recipients will see the message and all other email addresses that have received the message. On the other hand, Bcc stands for Blind Carbon Copy. If you use Bcc option to send a message to many recipients, all the recipients will see the message, but will not see other email addresses that have received the message.

- If you have more than one email account configured on the Email app and you wish to send from a different email account, tap the dropdown icon ▼ next to **From** and choose a different email account. See the picture below.

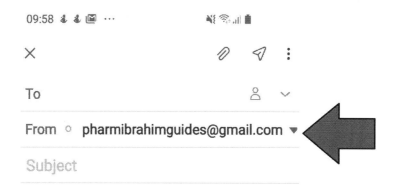

- Tap **Subject** field and key in the subject of your email.
- Tap the text input field and write the text for your email.

- You can use the formatting tab at the bottom of the screen to perform the following actions:

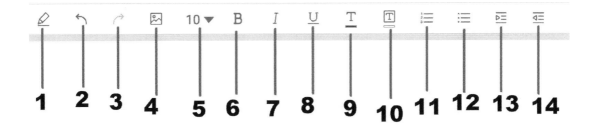

1. **Pen mode:** When you tap this icon, a writing pad would appear. Simply pick a writing color and begin to write your thoughts using the white pad that appears. When you are done, tap **Done** to save.

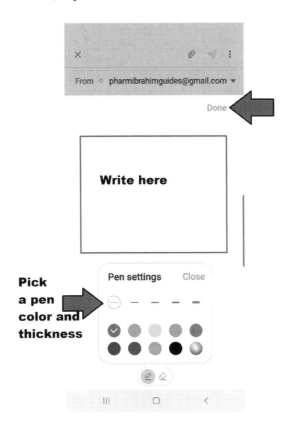

2. **Undo:** Tap to undo an action.

3. **Redo:** Tap to redo an action.

4. **Image:** Tap this to add an image.

5. **Font Size**: Use this option to change the font size of your text.

6. **Bold**: You can bolden a part or your entire message. To bolden a text, select the text(s) and tap the **B** icon.

7. **Italicize**: You can make your text appear italicized by clicking on the *I* icon.

8. **Underline**: Use the U icon to underline a text.

9. **Font color**: Tap this to change the font color.

10. **Font background color**: Tap this to change the font background color.

11. **Numbering**: Tap this to create a numbered list.

12. **Bullets**: Tap this to create a bulleted list.

13. **Increase indent**: Tap this to move the paragraph farther away from the margin.

14. **Decrease indent**: Tap this to move the paragraph towards the margin.

To access more formatting options, swipe the formatting icons to the left or right. (See the arrows below).

- When you are satisfied with the message and you are ready to send it, tap Send icon located at the top of the Email app screen.

Note: Before you can apply some of the formatting options above to a block of texts, you would need to select the texts. To do this, tap and hold a word and drag ⬤ or ⬤ to select the texts you want.

Tip: To save a message as draft, click on the menu icon ⋮ located at the top of the screen and select **Save in Drafts**. To access **Drafts** folder, open the Email app and swipe in from the left edge of the screen. Then tap **Drafts**.

Attaching a file

You can insert an attachment into your message by clicking on attach icon 📎 located at the top of the screen. Select the file type. Locate and tap on the file you want to attach. Tap **Done**.

To view saved/downloaded attachments, go to app screen and tap **Samsung** folder. Tap **My files** and tap an appropriate content category. Alternatively, visit **Photos/Gallery** app if the attachment is an image.

Managing a Received Email

One of the most important functions of any email app is the ability to receive incoming messages. By default, Email app searches for new messages and alerts you when there is one.

New messages are either stored in Inbox or Spam folder and these are the two places to check if you are expecting an email. To access **Spam** folder, open the Email app and swipe in from the left edge of the screen (or tap the menu icon ≡ found at the top of the screen). Then tap on **All Folders** and select **Spam**.

To see if there is a new message, open the Email app and swipe down from the top of the screen.

If you are not getting notifications from Email app, these are the things to check:

1. Check that you have not blocked notifications from this app. You can know this by following the steps on page 93-95.

2. Confirm that you have not disabled **Sync** function. To do this, swipe down from the top of the screen with two fingers. Then swipe left and see if **Sync** appears bold. If it appears bold, then it is enabled. Please note that if *Sync* is disabled you may not get some notifications.

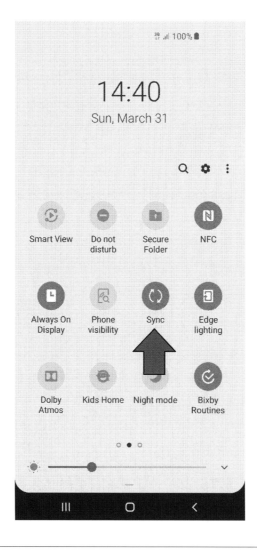

3. If the first two steps above do not work, then make sure your phone is not restricting the Email app's battery usage. Restricting the battery usage for Email app may affect its ability to get sync or use data. To know if Email app has a restricted battery usage, go to **Settings** ⚙ > **Apps** > **menu icon** ⋮ (located at the top of the screen) > **Special access** > **Optimize battery usage**. Tap the dropdown menu and select **All**.

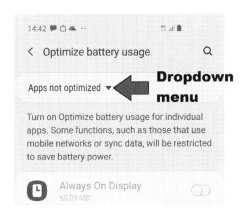 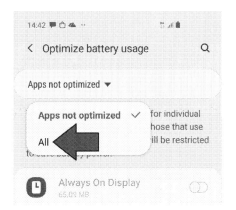

Scroll down and locate the **Email** app and make sure the indicator switch next to it is turned off.

To read a message:

- Tap on the subject of a message to open the message text in the preview pane.

- Those messages that you have not yet read should appear bold.

- A paperclip icon 📎 means that a message has an attachment.

- The Email app allows you to perform the following actions on a message in your inbox:

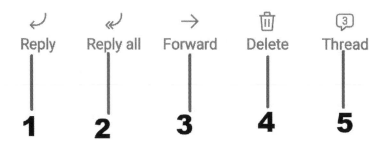

Reply	Reply all	Forward	Delete	Thread
1	**2**	**3**	**4**	**5**

If the icons above are not showing up while viewing an email message, swipe down from the middle of the screen.

1. **Reply:** Tap this button to reply an email message. When you tap this button, a new window appears. This window is similar to what appears when you tap on a new email button but with a slight difference. The reply window already contains the recipient's name and the subject (the subject line is preceded by "Re:"). In addition, the original message usually appears at the bottom of your reply for reference.

2. **Reply All:** If the message in your inbox is addressed to several people, you can choose to reply all those people by tapping **Reply All.** You may know whether an email is sent to many people by tapping **Details** tab next to the sender's name/address.

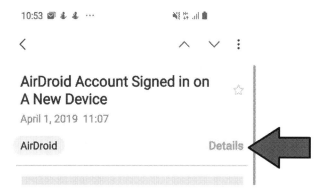

3. **Forward:** Use this option to send a copy of an email in your inbox to your friends or associates. When you tap on the **Forward** button, a message

window with a subject line preceded by "Fwd:" appears. The original message address (To and From), date, subject, attachment, and text are also usually included. In addition, you will have the option to fill in the email address of the person to whom you are sending the message.

4. **Delete:** Use this option to delete a message from your inbox. Alternatively, tap and hold the email and select **Delete.**

5. **Thread:** This shows the number of conversations you have made. To see the list of conversations, tap this icon.

Tip: When you open the Email app inbox to check a mail, the name of the sender is usually displayed on the top of the message pane. To copy the email address of whoever sent the message, tap the email and tap the name of the sender. Select **Copy email address**.

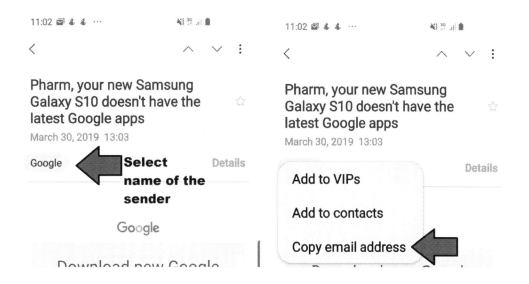

In addition, you could add the email address to your contact by selecting **Add to contacts**. To add an email address to VIP list, select **Add to VIPs**.

How to Open and Save an Attachment in the Email App

The email with an attachment will have a paper clip icon ✏ displayed next to the address of the sender when you check your message inbox.

To open an attachment:

1. Tap the message that has the attachment as indicated by a paper clip icon ✏.

2. When the message opens, tap **Save** next to the attachment to save it. If the attachment is more than one, select the drop-down arrow ∨ and then select "Save All" (if needed).

If your device does not have an appropriate program to open the attachment, you may be unable to view the attachment. In a situation like this, you would need to install the appropriate program for the file type. You may ask the person that sent the message about the appropriate program to use in opening the attachment.

3. To view saved attachments, go to the app screen and tap **Samsung** folder. Tap **My files** and tap **Downloads.** Alternatively, if the attachment is an image, go to **Photos/Gallery** app.

Managing the Settings Options

- To access the Email app settings, open the Email app and swipe in from the left edge of the screen.

- Tap on **Settings** located at the top of the screen.

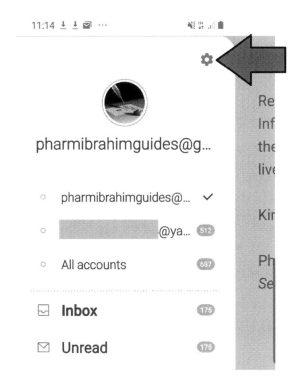

- Under **General** tab, tap an option.

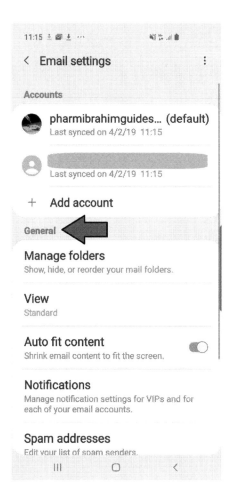

- To configure specific settings for an account, tap the account.
- To delete an account from your device, tap the email account and tap **REMOVE** next to the account name at the top of the screen.
- To manage what name appears when you send a message using the Samsung Email app, tap **Your name** and enter appropriate name. Then tap **Done**.

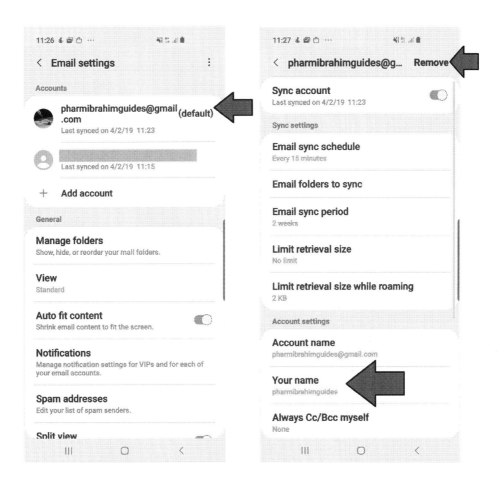

How to Remove the Default Email Signature in the Email App

You can use the Signature tab to tell the Email app what signature to include in a message. To do this, open the Email app, swipe in from the left edge of the screen and tap **Settings**

. Tap the desired account, tap **Signature** and key in a signature of your choice. Tap **Save** located at the top of the screen. You can use the switch next to Signature to enable or disable this feature.

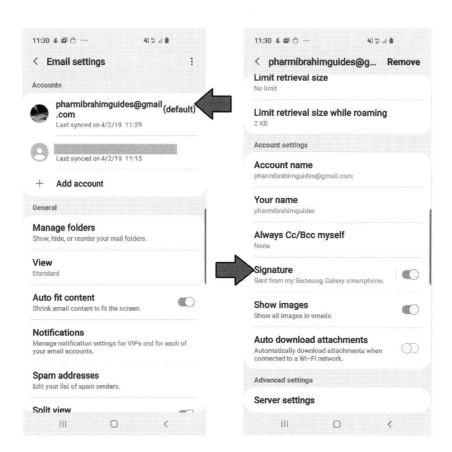

Note: An email signature is a text that appears by default after the body of your message. You may set your email signature to be your name or brand.

Gmail App Demystified

Gmail gives you many features that makes it special. In this manual, you would learn how to use Gmail app like a pro. Let's get started!

How to Add Your Email Accounts to the Gmail App

You probably have many email accounts and you may wish to add these accounts to the Gmail app.

To add an email account:

1. From the Home/App screen, tap **Google** and then **Gmail** . If you are using the app for the first time, please follow the prompts.
   If needed, you can download **Gmail** app from Google Play store.
2. To add your email account, tap "Add email address", "Take me to Gmail" or "Add another email address" and enter your email account information.
3. To add another email account, swipe in from the left edge of the screen, scroll down and tap **Settings**.

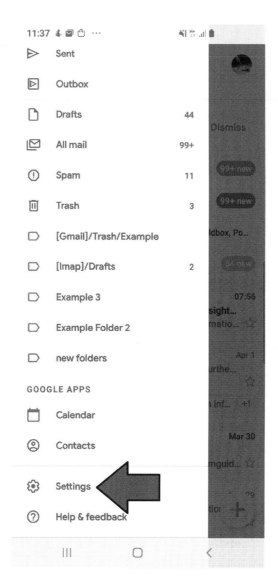

- Tap **Add account** and follow the prompts.

How to Compose and Send an Email Message Using Gmail App

You can easily send an email message to your friends or business colleagues using the Gmail app. In this section, we would be exploring how to compose and send an email message.

To compose and send an email message:

- From the Home screen, swipe up and tap **Google** and then **Gmail** .

- To change to another email account if multiple email accounts are configured, tap the profile picture of the current account and then tap the account you want to view.

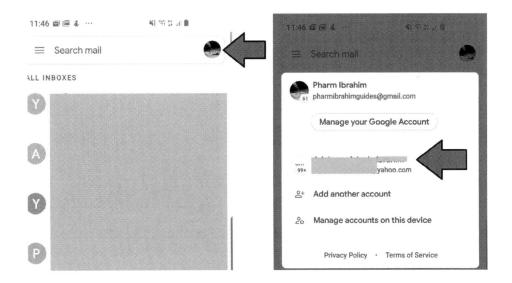

- To access a combined inbox of all the email accounts associated with Gmail app, tap the menu icon ☰ located at the top of the screen and select **All inboxes**.

- To compose a new email, tap the new email icon ⊕ located at the bottom of the screen.

- Tap the field next to the "**To**" field and type in the email address of the recipient. If enabled, as you type an email address, Gmail will suggest email addresses based on your contacts. To add another email address, simply type the email address into the "To" field. You may separate each email address with a coma. To delete/remove an email address from the "To" field, tap the email address and tap the **X** icon.

- To send a copy to another person, tap the dropdown icon $\vee$ next to the "**To**" field and type the person's email address in the **Cc/Bcc** field.

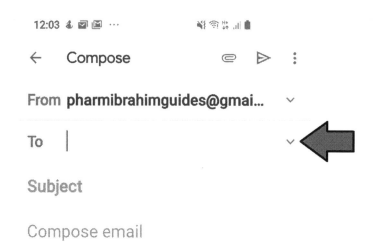

To know what Cc and Bcc stands for, please refer to the tip on page 253.

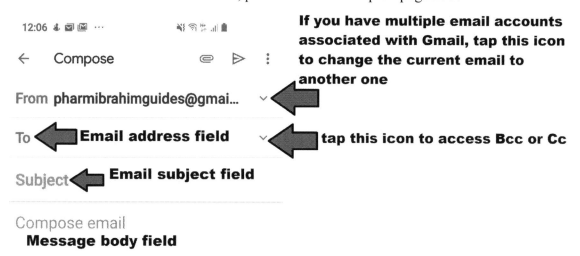

- If you have more than one email account configured on Gmail app and you wish to send from a different email account, tap the dropdown icon next to "**From**" to choose a different email account. See the picture above.
- Tap **Subject** field and key in the subject of your email.
- Tap the text input field and type the texts for your email. Writing suggestions appear in the message field as you type. To accept these suggestions, swipe right.

- To format a block of texts, select the texts by tapping and holding a word and drag 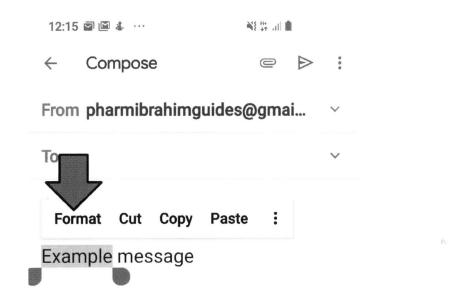 or ⬤ to select the texts you want. Then select **Format** from the options that appear.

You can use the formatting tab at the bottom of the screen to perform the following actions:

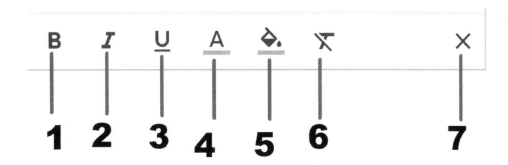

1. **Bold**: You can bolden a part or your entire message using this feature. To bolden a text, select the text(s) and tap the **B** icon.
2. **Italicize**: You can make your text appear italicized by clicking on the *I* icon.
3. **Underline**: Use the U icon to underline a text.
4. **Font color**: Tap this to change the font color.

5. **Font background color**: Tap this to change the font background color.

6. **Remove Formatting:** Tap this to remove any format you have given to a text or block of texts.

7. **Close:** Tap this to close the formatting dialogue box.

- When you are satisfied with the message and you are ready to send it, tap

   Send ▷ located at the top of the Gmail app screen.

- To save a message as draft, tap the menu icon ⋮ located at the top of the screen and select **Save Draft**. Please note that you may need to fill the "**To**" field or the body of the message before you can save a message as draft. On the other hand, to discard a message, tap the menu icon ⋮ and select **Discard**.

Note: Before you can apply some of the formatting options above to a block of texts, you would need to select the texts. To do this, tap and hold a word, then drag ◖ or ◗ to select the texts you want.

Attaching a File

You can insert an attachment into your message by clicking on the attachment icon ℘ located at the top of the screen. This opens a dialog box. Choose from **Attach file** or **Insert from Drive**. Then locate and tap on the file you want to attach.

Managing a Received Email

One of the most important functions of any email app is the ability to receive incoming messages. By default, Gmail app searches for new messages and alerts you when there is a message(s).

New messages are either stored in Inbox or Spam folder and these are the places to check

if you are expecting an email. To access Spam folder, tap the menu icon ☰, scroll down

and tap **Spam** folder. Alternatively, swipe from the left edge of the screen towards the

middle to access Spam folder.

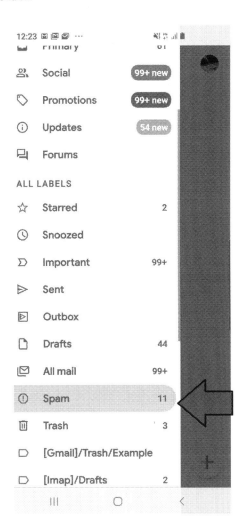

To see if there is a new message, swipe down from the top of the Gmail app's screen.

To read/manage a message:

Please note that some options discussed below might not be available on your phone. The options you see are dependent on the type of email account you are using. I have noticed that you will see a more robust set of options when you are using a Gmail account with Gmail app.

- Tap the subject of the message to open the message text in the preview pane.

- Unread messages should appear bold.

- The attachment icon means that a message has an attachment.

- To make a message your favorite, tap the star icon located at the top right corner of the screen.

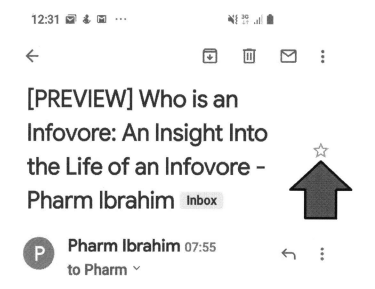

- To reply a message, scroll down on the message (if necessary) and tap **Reply**. If the email was sent to more than one person, you can tap **Reply all** to send the reply to all those who have received the message. To forward the message, tap

    Forward. While composing a reply message, you can tap the menu icon ⋮

(located at the top of the screen) to discard a message, save a message as draft or add an email address from the Contact app.

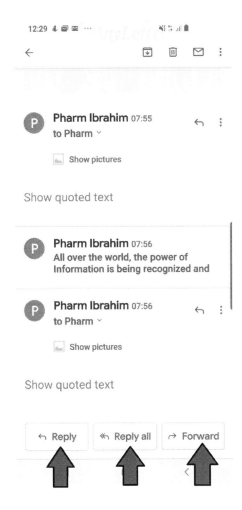

- To quickly delete a message, tap the delete icon located at the top of the screen.

- To move a message to another folder, tap the menu icon and select **Move to**. Then select the folder.

- To archive a message, tap the archive icon located at the top of the screen. To access archived messages, tap the menu icon ≡ (located at the top left corner of the screen) and tap **All mail**. Please note that when you archive a message, the message should come back to your inbox when someone replies.

- To access the details of a sender of an email, tap **to me** next to the sender's name. This allows you to see details like email address.

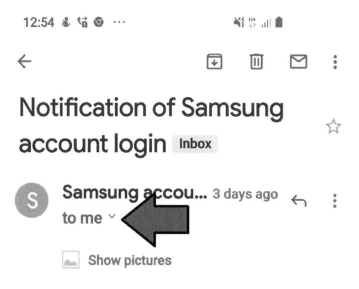

- To go back to inbox, while viewing a message, tap the inbox icon ✉.

Tip: You might like to customize what happens when you swipe the screen while viewing the message list in your inbox. To do this, please refer to the tip on page 291-292.

Using the Gmail In-App Inbox Menu icons

When you tap a message in your inbox, you will usually see two menu icons. These icons allow you to customize your messages. To access these menu icons,

- Open the Gmail app and tap a message from your inbox.
- Tap a menu icon (see the picture below).

Tap the first menu icon to access the following:

Please note that the options you see when you tap the menu icon is dependent on the type of email account you are using. I have noticed that you will see a more robust options when you are using a Gmail account. For example, when you add a Yahoo account, you would see less options.

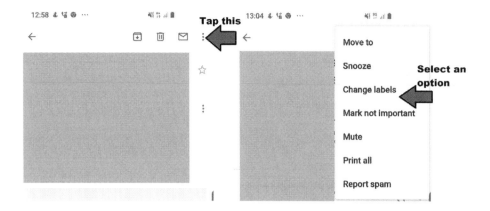

1. **Move to:** Choose this option to move an email to another folder.

2. **Snooze:** When you tap "Snooze", you will be able to hide the message concerned in *Snoozed* folder for a period of time. When you snooze a message, it is removed from the inbox and put inside the "snoozed" folder for a chosen time. To access Snoozed folder, if needed, tap the back arrow icon ← (located at the top of the screen) and tap the menu icon ☰ (located at the top left corner of the screen). Then tap **Snoozed**.

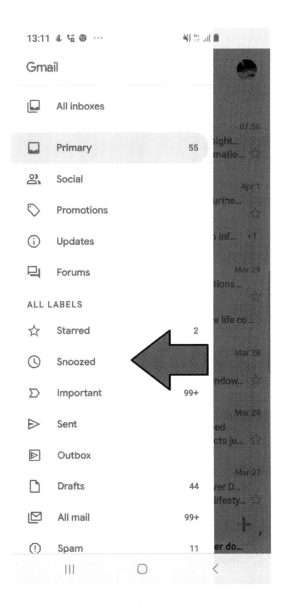

To unsnooze, open the Snoozed folder, tap the message you want to unsnooze and tap

the menu icon ⋮ . Then tap **Unsnooze.** *A snoozed email message should appear at the top of your emails after the snooze time elapses.*

Please note that you may not be able to use Snooze option if you are not using a Gmail account.

3. **Change labels:** When you change the label of an email, you move/copy the email to a new location. To change a label, select **Change labels** and tick a folder you like (you can uncheck the label you don't want). Then tap **OK.**

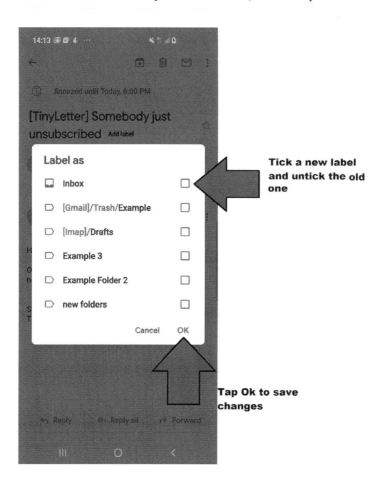

4. **Mark Important/Not Important:** Any message you find very dear to you, mark it as important. To mark a message as important, tap **Mark Important**. To access "Important" folder, tap the back arrow ← (if needed) and tap the menu icon ≡. Then tap **Important**. You could also mark a message as "not important" using this method.

5. **Unsubscribe**: Gmail app allows you to unsubscribe from some emails using this option. To unsubscribe from an email list, simply tap **Unsubscribe**. Tap **Unsubscribe** again to confirm.

6. **Mute:** You can mute a message to prevent it from appearing in your main inbox. To access your muted messages, tap the menu icon ☰. Tap **All mail**. Please note that when you mute a message, the message may not come back to your inbox when someone replies.

7. **Print:** Use this option to print an email or save an email as a PDF. To use this option to save an email as PDF, tap **Print.** Tap the dropdown arrow and select **Save as PDF** (if needed). Thereafter, tap the yellow **PDF** icon and choose a folder. Then tap **Done** to download.

To locate the file you just downloaded, go to **Samsung** folder > **My Files** > **Internal storage**. Then tap on the folder where you stored the downloaded file. If needed, tap the downloaded PDF file to open it.

8. **Revert auto-sizing:** If you are viewing an email in your inbox and it is not appearing as it should, you can tap on **Revert auto-sizing** to see if this solves the problem. *Note that this option is not always available.*

9. **Report Spam:** If you believe that an email message is a spam, you can report it to Google using this option.

Tap the second menu icon ⋮ to access the following:

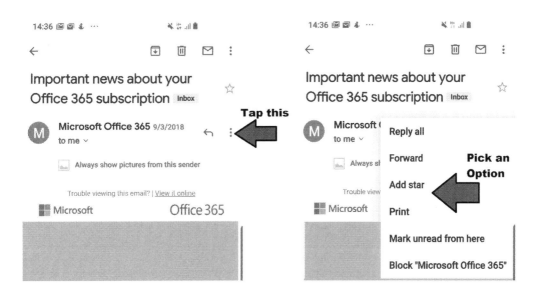

Please note that the options you see when you tap the (second) menu icon is dependent on the type of email account you are using. I have noticed that you will see a more robust set of options when you are using a Gmail account.

- **Reply all**: If an email is sent to more than one person, you can tap **Reply all** to reply to all those who have received the message.
- **Forward**: Select this option to forward a message to another person.
- **Add star (Make an email message your favorite)**: If you want to make a message your favorite, tap **Add star**. To view your starred message, tap the back arrow ← (located at the top of the screen) and tap the menu icon ≡ (located at the top left corner of the screen). Tap **Starred**.
- **Print:** Please refer to page 281 to learn how to manage print options.
- **Mark unread from here**: If you want a message to appear bold (as if it is unread), tap "Mark unread from here".
- **Block…**: If you don't want future messages from a contact to be delivered to your inbox, tap **Block…**
  Please note that any future message from a blocked contact will be marked as spam. To unblock a contact, tap the menu icon ⋮ again and select **Unblock…**

How to Open and Save an Attachment in Gmail App

The email with an attachment should have a paperclip icon 📎 displayed next to the address of the sender when you check your message inbox. Please note that Gmail app might also display the name of the attachment instead of the paperclip. See the picture below.

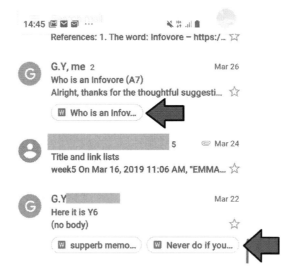

To open/manage an attachment:

1. Tap the message that has the attachment.

2. When the message opens, tap download icon ⬇ next to the attachment to download it.

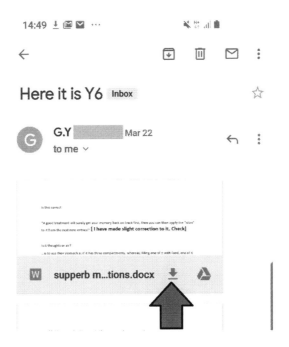

After the download, swipe down from the top of the screen and tap on the downloaded file to open it.

3. To view the attachment, simply tap it. If your device does not have an appropriate program to open the attachment, you may be unable to view the attachment. In a situation like this, you would need to install the appropriate app for the file type. You may ask the person that sent the message about the appropriate program to use in opening the attachment.

4. To view saved/downloaded attachments, go to applications screen and tap **Samsung** folder. Then tap **My Files** and select **Download**. Alternatively, you can double-tap the status bar (the bar at the top of the screen where icons such as Wi-Fi icon usually appear) to view your recent downloads. Then tap the downloaded file you want to view.

Tip: If you want a smart file management app on your phone, you may consider installing **Files by Google** from Google Play store.

In addition, you can prevent Gmail from automatically downloading an attachment when connected to Wi-Fi. To do this:

1. Open the Gmail app.

2. Tap the menu icon ≡ (located at the top left corner of the screen).

3. Scroll down the email options and tap **Settings.**

4. Tap an email account.

5. Scroll down and uncheck the box next to **Download attachments.**

Unsubscribing from an Email List

If you will like to unsubscribe from any email list, please follow the steps highlighted below:

- Open the message you want to unsubscribe from.

- Tap the menu icon ⋮ .

- Select **Unsubscribe.**
- Tap **Unsubscribe** again to confirm.

Blocking an email address

If an email address is disturbing you with unwanted emails, you can block the email address. To do this:

- Open the message in question.
- Tap the menu icon ⋮ .

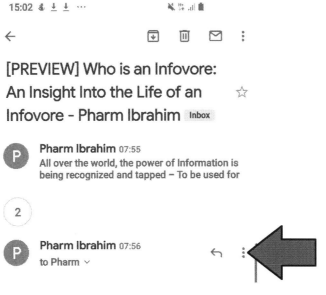

- Select **Block...**

Please note that any future message from a blocked contact will be marked as spam. To unblock a contact, tap the menu icon ⋮ again and select **Unblock...**

Cleaning Up Your Inbox

Overtime, inbox usually grows to contain thousands of irrelevant messages. If this is your situation and you wish to clean your inbox so that it contains only the most important messages, please follow the instructions below:

1. Open the Gmail app and look for those emails that contain the most irrelevant/unwanted messages. Open one of these emails and block the sender's address. Repeat this step for all the annoying email messages. Please see page 287 to know how to block a sender.

2. Then go back to your inbox and select all the irrelevant/unwanted messages. To select a message, tap and hold the message for one second and lift your finger. Repeat this method to select all the irrelevant/unwanted messages. If you mistakenly select a message, tap and hold the message for one second and lift your finger to unselect it. Then tap the delete icon 🗑 (located at the top of the screen) to send the selected messages to the Trash folder. *Please note that items that have been in Trash folder for more than 30 days will be deleted (automatically).*

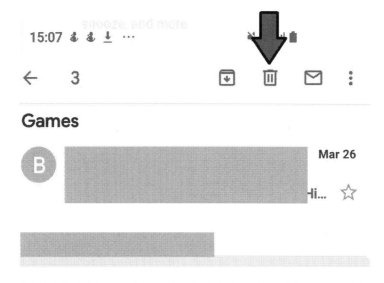

3. Go back to your inbox and select all the very important messages following the method mentioned in step 2. Then tap the menu icon ⋮ (located at the top of the screen) and select **Mark important**. To access "Important" folder, tap the menu icon ☰ and tap **Important**. Please note that if you mark a message as important, the message should remain in your primary inbox.

4. Go back to your inbox and select all social/promotional messages following the method mentioned in step 2. Then tap the menu icon ⋮ (located at the top of the screen) and select **Move to**. Select **Social** or **Promotions**. To access Social or Promotions folder, tap the menu icon ☰ and tap **Social/Promotions**.

5. Finally, go back to your inbox and tap the menu icon ☰. Scroll down, tap **Settings** and tap an account. Then tap **Inbox categories**. Make sure the checkbox next to **Update** is selected. When this is selected, Gmail will automatically put auto-generated updates including receipts, bills and statements in Updates folder. This should allow you to find your bills and statements faster in the future. Make sure **Social** and **Promotions** folders are also selected. You may also check the box next to **Forums** if you want messages from online groups, discussion boards and mailing lists to be put in one folder.

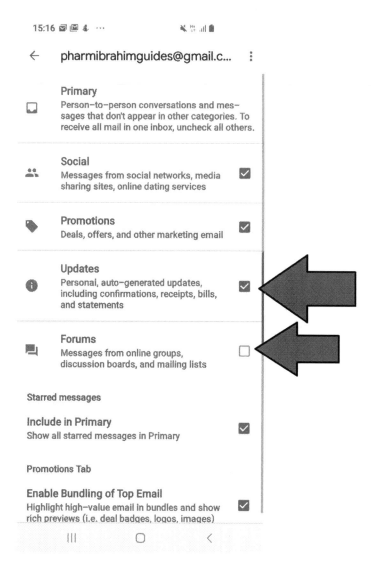

After doing all the five steps highlighted above, you would see that your **Primary** folder would contain fewer messages (because some of the messages would have been moved to **Updates, Forum**, **Social** and **Promotions** folders).

Please note that, if you have several thousands of emails, it may take time before you can clean up your inbox. If this is your situation, I would advise you clean up your inbox gradually so as not to be overwhelmed. In addition, if you can, make sure you decide the fate of your future messages within 72 hours of receiving. Try to delete an unwanted message as soon as you read it. Don't wait for it to become a concern before you send a useless message to the trash bin.

Tip: You might like to customize what happens when you swipe the screen while viewing conversation list in your inbox, to do this:

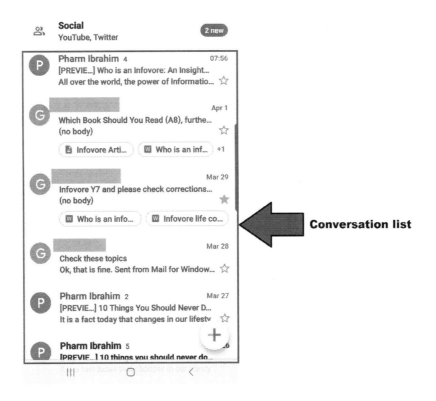

1. Open the Gmail app and tap the menu icon ☰. Tap on **Settings**.
2. Tap **General settings**.
3. Tap **Swipe actions**.
4. Tap **Change** next to **Right swipe** and pick an option.

5. Tap **Change** next to **Left swipe** and pick an option.

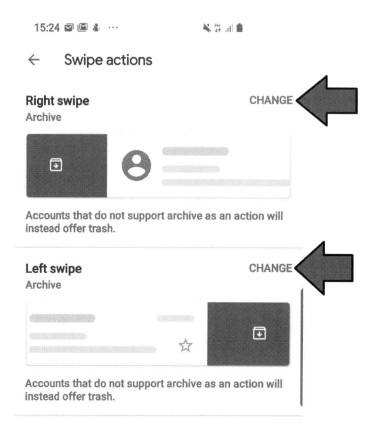

Searching the Gmail App

To avoid wasting time, you can use the search option in the Gmail app to quickly find emails. When looking for an email, using the search tab is usually the best option if you know the right search phrase to use.

To use the search feature:

1. Open the Gmail app.
2. Tap the **Search mail** (located at the top of the screen).

3. Enter a search phrase and tap the lens icon or the "Done" button on the on-screen keyboard.

To delete your Gmail search history:

1. Open the Gmail app.

2. Tap the menu icon ☰.

3. Scroll down and tap **Settings.**

4. Tap **General settings.**

5. Tap the menu icon ⋮ (located at the top of the screen).

6. Tap **Clear search history**.

Stop Picture from Being Automatically Displayed

If you have allowed images to be displayed from a sender while viewing an email message, you can follow the steps mentioned below to revoke this approval.

1. Repeat steps 1 to 5 under "To delete your Gmail search history" above.

2. Tap **Clear picture approvals**.

Tip: You can prevent images from being shown inside your email messages. To do this, repeat steps 1 to 3 under "To delete your Gmail search history" above. Tap an email account, then scroll down and tap **Images**. Select **Ask before displaying external images**.

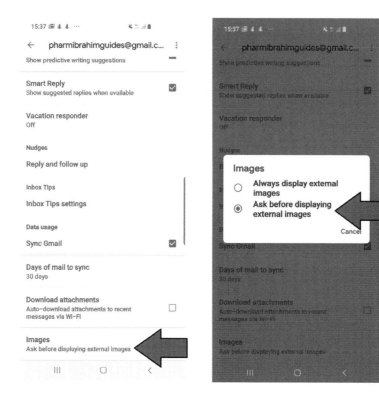

Using Vacation Responder

If you are on a vacation, you can enable Gmail to auto-respond to people that message you during this time.

Please note that the Vacation Responder might not be available if you are not using a Gmail account.

In addition, normally, messages categorized as spam and messages addressed to mailing list (you subscribe to) won't get response from the vacation responder.

To use vacation responder:

1. Open the Gmail app.

2. Tap the menu icon ☰ (located at the top left corner of the screen).

3. Scroll down the email options and tap **Settings**.

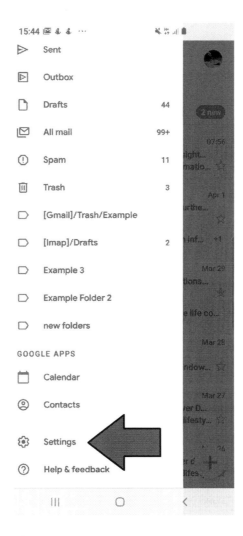

4. Tap an email account.

5. Tap **Vacation responder**.

6. Tap the status switch next to **Vacation responder** and fill in necessary information.

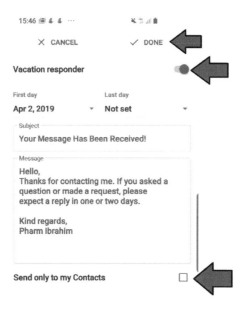

7. If you want Gmail to message only your contacts, tap the checkbox next to **Send only to my Contacts**.

8. Tap **Done** located at the top of the screen to save the changes.

9. To deactivate Vacation Responder, repeat steps 1 to 6 above, and tap the switch next to **Vacation Responder**.

Managing the Settings Options

Some of the options under Email Settings have already been discussed. But I would like to briefly mention a few more things.

1. To access the Email app settings, open the Gmail app and tap the menu icon (located at the top left corner of the screen). Tap on **Settings**.

2. Tap an email account and tap an option of your choice. For example, to disable email notification, tap **Notifications** and then select **None**.

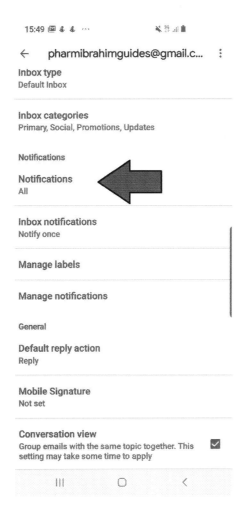

Tip: You might notice that if you tap on weblinks while reading an email, it opens in Gmail app. If you want to disable this feature so that the weblink can be opened using a web browser, perform the following actions:

a. Open the Gmail app and tap the menu icon ☰. Tap on **Settings**.
b. Tap **General settings**.
c. Uncheck the box next to **Open web links in Gmail**.

Also, if you want Gmail to prompt you before deleting, archiving, or sending a message, then tick the appropriate box. See the picture above.

Removing Your Email Account from Gmail App

To remove your email account:

1. Swipe down from the top of the screen and select settings icon 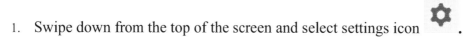.

2. Tap **Accounts and backup**.

3. Tap **Account**.

4. Select the (Google) account you want to remove.

5. Tap **Remove Account**. Select **Remove Account** to confirm your choice.

Managing Email Signature

You can use the Signature tab to tell Gmail app what signature to include in a message. You can also edit signature message under this tab. To go to Signature settings, open the Gmail app and tap the menu icon ☰. Scroll down and tap on **Settings**. Tap the desired account and tap **Mobile signature**. Type in the signature you want and tap **OK.**

Tip: An email signature is a text that appears by default after the body of your message. You may set your email signature to be your name or your brand.

Personal Information

Contacts

This app allows you to create and manage a list of your personal or business contacts. You can save names, mobile phone numbers, home phone numbers, email addresses and more.

Creating a contact

1. While on the Home screen, swipe up and tap on **Contact**  app. If you are using the Contacts app for the first time, follow the onscreen instructions to set it up.

2. Tap on **Add contact** icon located at the lower right corner of the screen.

3. Select where you want to save the contact from the options that appear. To make your selection the default selection, tap **Set as Default.**

To change your selection afterward, tap the dropdown arrow next to your selection. See the picture below.

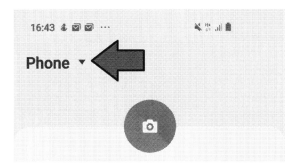

4. Fill in the details by tapping on each item/entry on the screen.
5. To assign a contact to a group, tap **Group.**
6. To access more options, tap on **View more**.

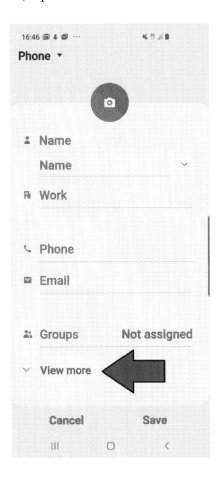

7. When you are done, tap **Save** located at the bottom of the screen.

Please note that if you choose SIM card as your storage location in step 3 above, you may not be able to fill more than a name and phone number.

Tip: To search for a contact, open the contact app and tap the search bar icon (located at the top of the screen) 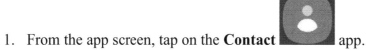. Start typing a name. The list filters as you type.

When you receive a message, you can easily save the number if it is not yet saved on your contacts list. To do this, tap the messaging app. Tap a conversation and tap **Add to contacts** (located at the top of the screen). Follow the on-screen instructions to finish the process.

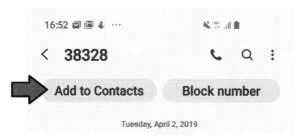

Troubleshooting hint: If you are unable to change the storage location when adding a new contact, do this. Swipe in from the left edge of the screen (or tap the menu icon ≡) and select **All contacts** (found at the top of the screen). Then try to add the new contact again. You should now be able to change the storage location for the contact.

Managing Contacts

1. From the app screen, tap on the **Contact** app.
2. Tap on a contact from the list.
3. To see the history of calls, messages, events with a contact, select **History**.
4. To edit a contact, tap **Edit** located at the bottom of the screen and enter the new details. Tap **Save** (found at the bottom of the screen) when you are done.

Tip: Please note that you might not be able to change the storage location of a contact using the editing option. If you need to change the storage location of a contact, I would recommend you consider copying the contact to the new location. To know how to copy a contact, please see page 306.

5. To delete a contact, open the contact app, tap and hold the contact you want to delete, then tap on **Delete** located at the bottom of the screen. You can also use this method to delete many contacts at once. Simply tap, hold and select all the contacts you want to delete, then tap **Delete**.

6. To share a contact, tap and hold the contact you want to share, then tap **Share.**

7. To link a contact, tap the contact and tap the menu icon ⋮ . Select **Link to another contacts**.

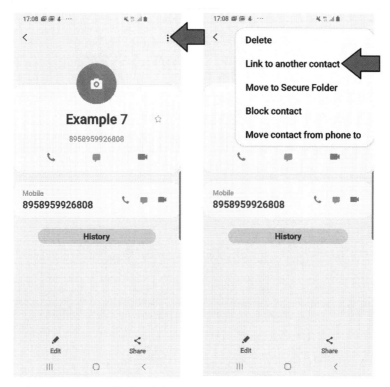

Then tap the contacts to link with. Tap **Link** (located at the bottom of the screen). Linking two contacts is important if you have separate entries for the same contact from different social networking services or email accounts.

8. To unlink a contact, tap the contact you want to unlink and tap the menu icon ⋮ . Tap **Add/remove linked contacts** and tap the **Unlink** next to the contact you want to unlink. To link another contact, tap **Link another contact**. If you have many contacts linked together, tap **Unlink all** (located at the bottom of the screen) to unlink all of them.

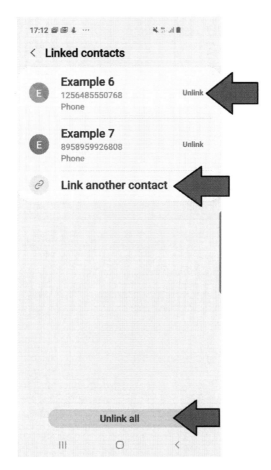

Please note that unlinking a contact does not delete the contact.

Tip: Do you want to see all the contacts stored on your phone or SIM, open the Contact app and swipe in from the left edge of the screen. Then tap **Phone** or **SIM** to view the contacts stored on it.

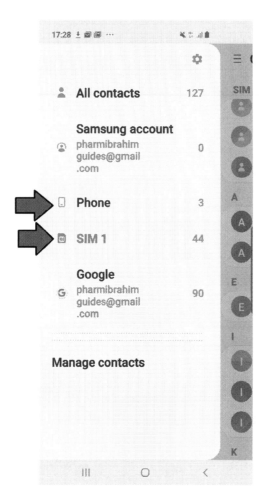

In addition, you can quickly call a contact by swiping right on it. To message a contact, swipe left.

Copy contact(s)

If you have some contacts stored on your SIM card, you can copy them to your phone with some simple steps.

1. From the app screen, tap on the **Contact** app.

2. Tap the menu icon found at the top part of the screen. Alternatively, swipe in from the left edge of the screen.

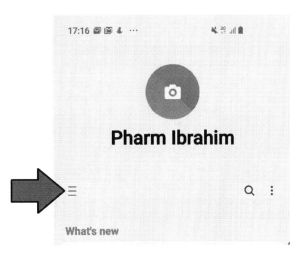

3. Tap **Manage contacts**.

4. Tap **Import/Export contacts**.

5. Tap **Import**.

6. Select where you want to copy the contact(s) from.

7. If you want to import all the contacts, tap **ALL** located at the top of the screen. You may also individually select the contacts by tapping them. To remove a contact you have previously selected, tap the minus icon next to it.

8. Tap **DONE** (located at the bottom of the screen).

9. Tap **Phone** or where you are sending the contacts to.

10. Tap **Import.** Please note that you can use this method to also copy contacts from SD card and internal storage.

Tip: You can **export** contacts from your phone to other places by following the steps similar to the ones mentioned above. But don't forget that you will select **Export** (and not Import) in step 5.

Contact Group

If you would like to send a message to several people at the same time, I would recommend that you create a contact group. You can create a contact group for friends, family members and business associates in order to reach them easily.

To create a group:

1. From the app screen, tap on the **Contact** app.
2. Swipe in from the left edge of the screen and tap **Groups**. Then tap **Create group.**

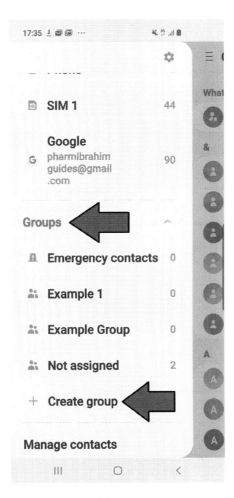

3. Fill in a name for the group, tap **Add member** to add members to the newly created group and tap **Done/Save**.

4. To remove a contact from a group, tap the minus icon next to the contact.

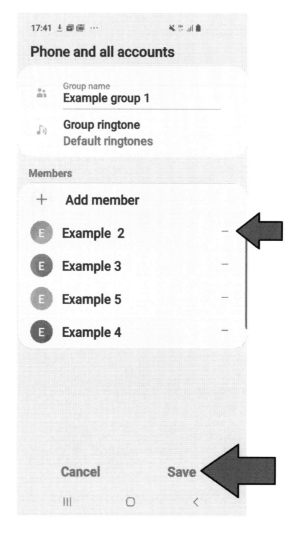

5. Tap **Save** (located at the bottom of the screen).

Please note that you may not be able to add contacts stored on SIM card to a contact group.

To add members to a group afterwards:

1. From the app screen, tap on **Contact** 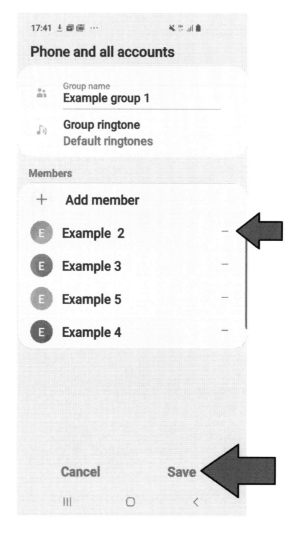 app.

2. Swipe in from the left edge of the screen, scroll down (if needed), tap on **Groups** and tap a group. You might also tap on the menu icon ☰ located at the top of the screen to access "Groups".

3. Tap the menu icon ⋮ and select **Edit group.**

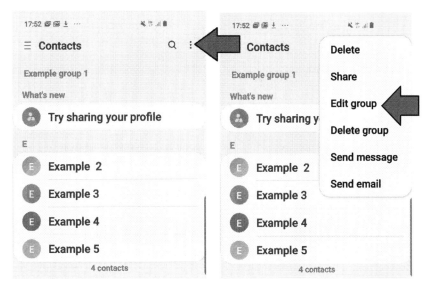

4. Tap **Add Member**. Then tap on the contacts to add and tap **Done**.

5. Tap **Save** (located at the bottom of the screen) to save the changes.

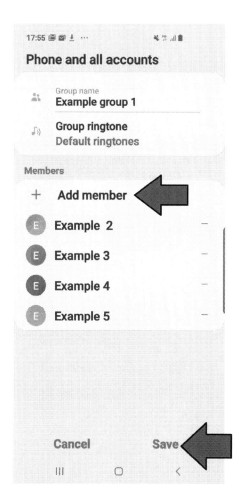

Tip: To remove a contact from a group, follow steps 1 to 3 above, then tap the minus icon  next to the contact you want to remove.

Managing a group contact:

1. From the app screen, tap on the **Contact** app.
2. Swipe in from the left edge of the screen, scroll down (if needed), tap on **Groups** and tap a group. You might also tap on the menu icon located at the top of the screen to access "Groups".

3. To send a message to a group, tap **Menu icon** ⋮ found at the top of the screen and tap **Send message**.

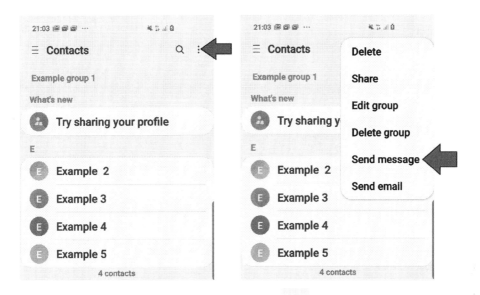

4. To send an email to a group, tap **Menu icon** ⋮ and tap **Send email**. Please note that you may not be able to send email to a group if you have not added email addresses to the individual contacts in the group.

Deleting a group:

1. Repeat steps 1 and 2 under **Managing a group contact**

2. Tap **Menu icon** ⋮ .

3. Tap **Delete group**.

4. Tap **Group only** to delete only the group. Tap **Group and members** to delete both the group and the contact(s) in the group.

Tip: To customize the Contact app, tap on the **Contact** app, swipe in from the left edge of the screen and select the settings icon. Then tap an option to customize.

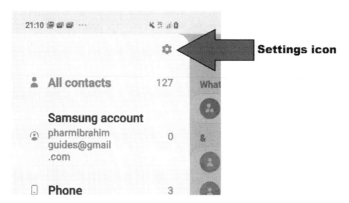

In addition, you can change the default storage for your contacts if need be. To do this:

1. From the app screen, tap on the **Contact** 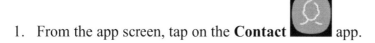 app.

2. Swipe in from the left edge of the screen or tap the menu icon ☰.

3. Tap **Manage contacts**.

4. Tap **Default storage location** and choose a new location.

Accessibility Features – the Special Features for Easy Usage

Accessibility services are special features for those with physical challenges. In addition, it provides you the opportunity to control your phone in a special way.

Screen reader

When this option is enabled, you would get voice feedback of what you tap, activate or select. This helps visually impaired people to interact with their phones.

To use Screen Reader:

1. Swipe down from the top of the screen and select the settings icon .
2. Scroll down and tap **Accessibility**.
3. Tap **Screen reader**.
4. Tap the status switch next to **Voice Assistant** to activate it.
5. Generally, when the Voice Assistant is turned on, you would need to tap once to select an item and double tap to activate/deactivate/explore the item.
   Use two fingers to scroll up/down or left/right.

Tip: To quickly turn off Screen Reader, simultaneously press volume up and down button for three-seven seconds.

Visibility enhancements

This option allows you to access vision related settings.

To use the visibility enhancements:

1. Swipe down from the top of the screen and select the settings icon .
2. Scroll down and tap **Accessibility**.
3. Tap **Visibility enhancements**.

4. Tap the desired option. Interestingly, for complex options, usually, there are explanations beneath them. You can read these explanations to get what each option represents.

Tip: Visibility enhancements tab contains those settings that help with vision. These settings are particularly good for visually impaired person.

Hearing enhancements

This tab allows you to control sound related settings. For example, you can turn off all sounds using this feature.

To use the Hearing enhancements:

1. Swipe down from the top of the screen and select the settings icon .
2. Scroll down and tap **Accessibility.**
3. Tap **Hearing enhancements.**
4. Tap the desired option. Interestingly, for complex options, usually, there are explanations beneath them. You can read these explanations to get what each option represents.

Tip: You can customize your phone to alert you when your baby is crying or when the doorbell is making a sound. This is a cool feature *but should be used responsibly*. To use this feature, repeat steps 1 to 3 under "To use the Hearing enhancements". Then tap **Sound detectors** and select an option. Carefully read the message that appears and follow the prompts to activate this feature.

Interaction and Dexterity

This option allows you to control your device in a special way. For example, you can control your device with your customized switches using the **Universal switches** tab. Although, I would advise you don't tamper with the **Universal switches** unless you know much about it. If you mistakenly switch on **Universal switches** and you wish to turn it off, just press the power button and the volume up button simultaneously once.

To use Interaction and dexterity:

1. Swipe down from the top of the screen and select the settings icon .
2. Scroll down and tap **Accessibility**.
3. Tap **Interaction and dexterity**.
4. Tap the desired option. Interestingly, for complex options, usually, there are explanations beneath them. You can read these explanations to get what each option represents.

Tip: Dexterity and interaction tab contains those settings that help you to control your device with gestures.

In addition, you can control how long you tap and hold the screen before you get a response. To do this, while in **Interaction and dexterity**, tap **Touch and hold delay** and choose an option.

Advanced settings

This option allows you to access extra accessibility settings. For example, you can turn on the flash notification if you want your phone to flash its light when there is a notification.

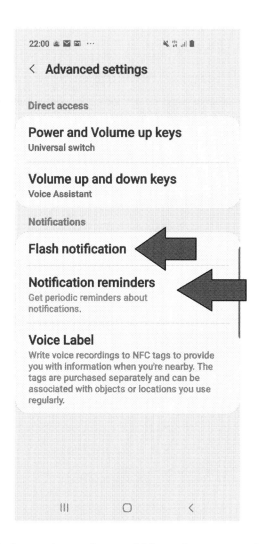

Tip: You can get reminded at a chosen interval if you have unread notifications. To do this, tap **Notification reminder** (see the picture above) and make sure the status switch is turned on. Then tap **Remind every** and choose an option. To control which app you receive notification from, tap **Selected apps** and then tap the status switch next to the individual app(s).

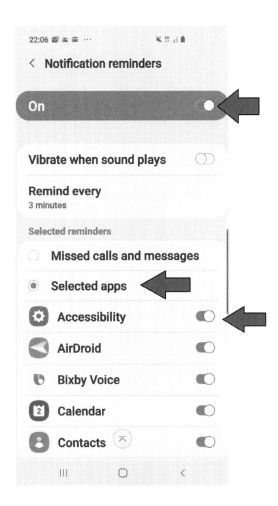

Installed Services

This tab allows you to access/manage additional accessibility app(s). Any accessibility app downloaded from Google Play store or Galaxy Apps should appear here.

TOOLS

Easy Mode

Easy mode provides a simpler layout and bigger icons on the Home/Apps screen, thereby enhancing visual experience and easier use. Please note that some features may not be available when Easy mode is enabled.

To enable and manage Easy mode:

1. Swipe down from the top of the screen and select the settings icon ⚙ . Tap **Display** tab.
2. Scroll down and tap **Easy mode**.
3. Tap **Easy mode** to enable this feature.
4. Tap **Apply** located at the bottom of the screen to save your settings. Then tap the Home button to return to the Home screen.
5. When Easy mode is enabled, you can add a shortcut to your favorite contacts. To add a shortcut to a contact, from the Home screen, swipe the screen to the right (you may need to swipe more than once). Then tap the plus icon and follow the prompts.

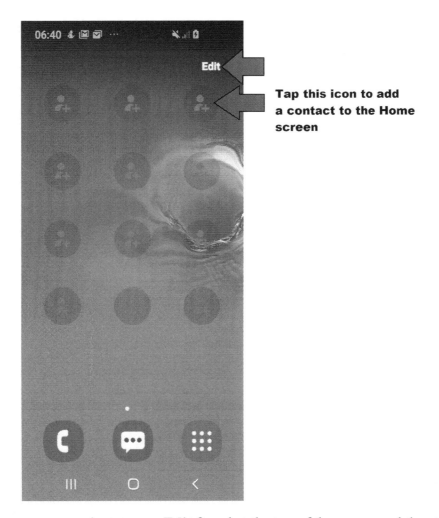

Tap this icon to add a contact to the Home screen

6. To remove a contact, tap on **Edit** found at the top of the screen and then tap the minus icon next to the contact you want to remove.

To disable Easy mode:

1. Swipe down from the top of the screen and select the settings icon ⚙ . Tap **Display** tab.
2. Scroll down and tap **Easy mode**.
3. Tap **Standard mode** to exit Easy mode.
4. Tap **Apply** to effect the changes.

Do Not Disturb

Do not disturb gives you the opportunity to prevent unnecessary disturbances from your phone. To quickly access this feature and customize it, swipe down from the top of the screen using two fingers, then tap and hold **Do Not disturb** for two seconds. Please note that you may need to swipe to the right to access more quick settings icons before you can see **Do Not disturb** icon.

Then select an option.

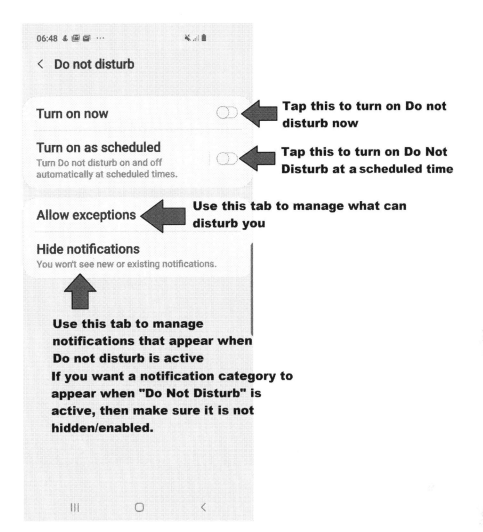

Tap this to turn on Do not disturb now

Tap this to turn on Do Not Disturb at a scheduled time

Use this tab to manage what can disturb you

Use this tab to manage notifications that appear when Do not disturb is active
If you want a notification category to appear when "Do Not Disturb" is active, then make sure it is not hidden/enabled.

If you choose to schedule Do Not Disturb, then use **Days** and **Set schedule** to customize your experience. Note that when a day is circled then it is selected. Thereafter, tap the back button to move back to the Do not disturb main settings page.

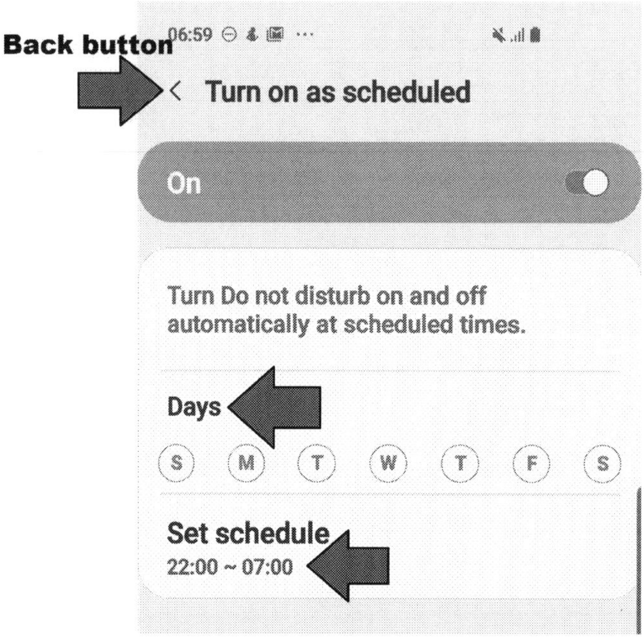
Back button
06:59
Turn on as scheduled
On
Turn Do not disturb on and off automatically at scheduled times.
Days
S M T W T F S
Set schedule
22:00 ~ 07:00

Tip: There is a feature on your phone called **Blue Light Filter**. Samsung claims this feature can help you sleep better. If you are having difficulty sleeping while using your phone, you may try using this feature. To use this feature:

Swipe down from the top of the screen and tap the settings icon  > **Display** > **Blue Light Filter** > **Turn on now**.

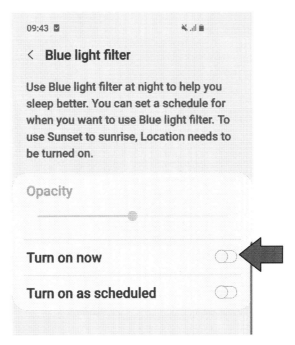

To schedule Blue Light Filter, tap the switch next to **Turn on as scheduled** and the choose an option.

Creating Schedules and More with the Calendar App

Your phone provides you with **Calendar** app to help you organize your schedules and tasks more conveniently and effectively. You can create schedules and add events.

Creating an event

5. From the Home screen, swipe up and tap on **Calendar** .

6. Tap the plus icon  at the lower right side of the screen and carefully enter the details.

7. To set the start and the end date of the event, tap **Start/End**. If the event is an All-day event, then tap on **All day**. To learn more about All day event, see page 336.

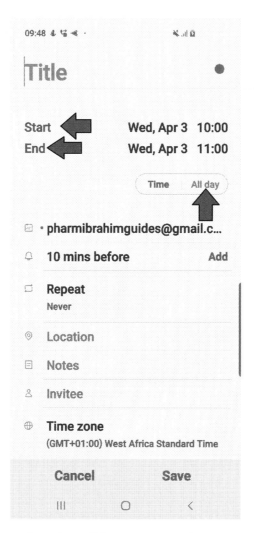

8. To change the storage location of the event, tap the storage location dropdown menu.

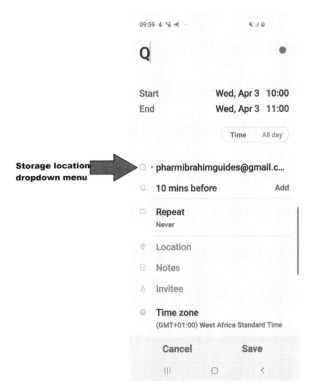

Storage location
dropdown menu

9. When you are done, tap **Save** (located at the bottom of the screen).

Tip: Your phone should give you a notification when the time for an event comes.

Changing your calendar view

1. From the Home screen, swipe up and tap on **Calendar** 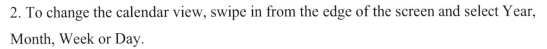.

2. To change the calendar view, swipe in from the edge of the screen and select Year, Month, Week or Day.

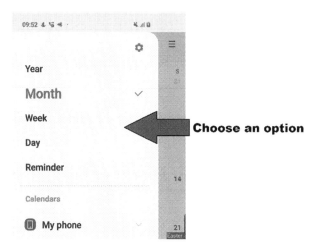

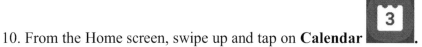

Choose an option

Viewing an event/schedule

10. From the Home screen, swipe up and tap on **Calendar** .

11. To change the calendar view, swipe in from the edge of the screen and select Year, Month, Week or Day.

12. Then tap on an event to view.

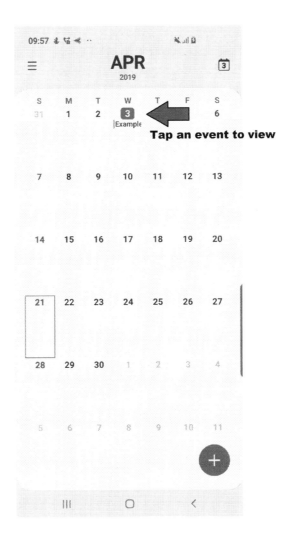

Tap an event to view

Editing, sharing or deleting an event

1. From the Home screen, swipe up and tap on **Calendar** ![calendar icon].

2. To change the calendar view, swipe in from the edge of the screen and select Year, Month, Week or Day.

3. To delete an event, tap on the event to open it, then tap and hold the event and select **Delete**.

4. To share an event, tap and hold the event and select **Share**.

5. To edit an event, tap and hold the event and select **Edit**.

Tip: To customize the Calendar app, from the Home screen, swipe up and tap **Calendar** . Swipe in from the left edge of the screen and select the settings icon (see the picture below). Choose an option.

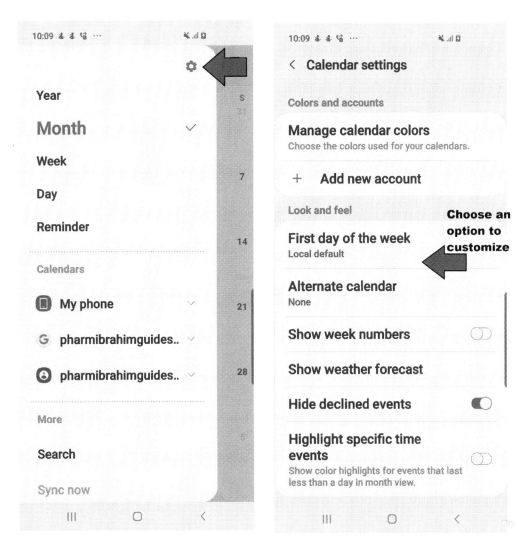

In addition, you can search the Calendar app for events. To do this, swipe in from the left edge of the screen and tap **Search**. Enter a keyword or phrase and tap the lens icon on the on-screen keyboard.

Google Calendar App

Google Calendar app helps you organize your schedules and tasks more conveniently and effectively. As at the time of writing this book, Google Calendar app has a more robust set of options than the Samsung Calendar app that comes with your device.

You can download Google Calendar app from Google Play store. In addition, if you have already added your Google account to your phone, the calendar events from this account should appear in the Google Calendar app.

If you have not added your Google account to your phone, you can do so by following these steps:

1. Swipe down from the top of the screen and select the settings icon .

2. Tap **Accounts and backup**.

3. Tap **Accounts**.

4. Tap **Add account.**

5. Tap **Google** and follow the prompts.

Creating an Event

1. From the Home screen, swipe up and tap on **Calendar** . If you are using the Calendar app for the first time, follow the on-screen instructions to set it up.

2. Tap the plus icon at the lower right side of the screen and choose whether you want to create a **goal**, a **reminder**, or an **event.** In this example, **event** is selected.

3. To set the start and end date/time of the event, tap the on-screen date/time and adjust them accordingly. If the event is an all-day event, tap the status switch next to **All-day** to activate it. When you activate all-day, you would not be able to set a specific time for your event. To learn more about all-day event, see page 336.

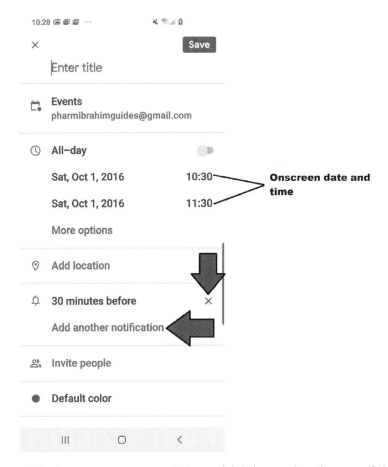

4. To enter a title for your event, tap "Enter title" located at the top of the screen and enter a title. Carefully fill in the other details. To choose when to receive notification for the event, tap on **Add another notification**. To remove a notification, tap on the **X** icon next to the notification (see the picture above).

5. When you are done, tap **Save** (located at the top of the screen).

Tip: Your phone should give you a notification when the time for an event arrives.

Creating a Reminder

1. From the home screen, swipe up and tap on **Calendar** .

2. Tap the plus icon 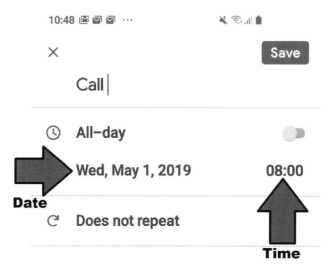 at the lower right side of the screen and choose **Reminder**.

3. Enter a title for your reminder. Tap **Done** on the virtual keyboard. If you don't want the reminder to be an **all-day** event (and you wish to set a specific time), tap the status switch next to **All-day** to deactivate it. When you deactivate all-day, you would be able to set a specific time.

4. Tap the date to adjust the date. Tap the time to adjust it.

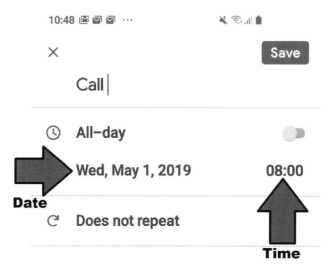

5. To choose when to repeat the reminder, tap **Does not repeat** and pick an option.

6. When you are done, tap **Save** (located at the top of the screen).

Creating a Goal

1. From the Home screen, swipe up and tap on **Calendar**.

2. Tap the plus icon at the lower right side of the screen and choose **Goal**.

3. Choose a goal and follow the onscreen instructions to complete the process.

4. To access more options, tap **More Options**. Tap the checkmark 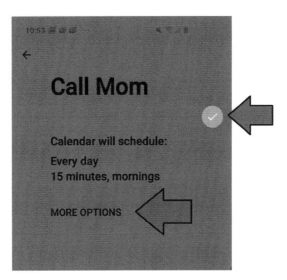 to save your goal.

5. Wait for the saving process to finish. If prompted, tap **Looks Good** if Google Calendar timing for your goal is OK, if not, tap **Adjust time**.

Tap the pen icon (found at the top of the screen), then tap the time and adjust it as you like.

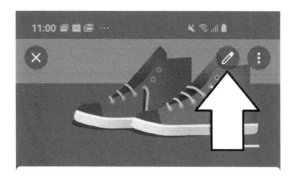

Finally, tap **Save** (located at the top of the screen) to save the changes.

Understanding All-day Event

All-day event is a type of event that will take a lot of hours to be completed. For example, if an event will begin by 9 a.m. and finish by 6 p.m., this type of event should be categorized as an all-day event. This would make it easier to see all other schedules (like reminders) happening during this time on your calendar. If you were to schedule an event between 9 a.m. and 6 p.m. on your calendar (and you don't select it as all-day event), it will block off a lot of time on your calendar. It may also overshadow other concurrent events.

In the picture below, the event is supposed to be an all-day event, but I have refused to do so.

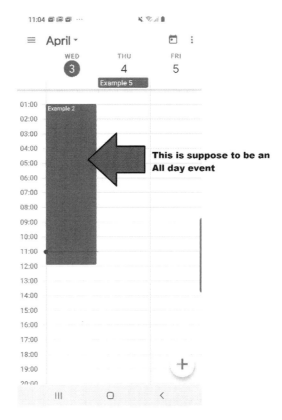

When I made the same event an all-day event, it becomes this (see below).

To make event an event an all-day event, please go to step 3 under **Creating an Event** (see page 332).

Changing Calendar View

1. From the Home screen, swipe up and tap on **Calendar** .

2. To change the calendar view, swipe in from the left edge of the screen (or tap the menu icon ≡ found at the top left corner of the screen) and select **Month**, **Week**, **3 Day** or **Day**.

Viewing an Event, Reminder or Goal

1. From the Home screen, swipe up and tap on **Calendar** .

2. To change the calendar view, tap the menu icon ≡ (found at the top left corner of the screen).

3. Select **Month**, **Week**, **3 Day** or **Day**.

4. Then tap on an event, reminder or goal to view.

Editing an Event, Reminder or Goal

1. Repeat steps 1 to 4 above.

2. Tap the pen icon ✏ (found at the top of the screen) and adjust what you want. Tap **Save** (located at the top of the screen) to save the changes.

Deleting an Event, Reminder or Goal

1. From the home screen, swipe up and tap on **Calendar** .

2. To change the calendar view, tap the menu icon ≡ (located at the top of the screen).

3. Select **Month**, **Week** or **Day**.

4. Then tap on an event, reminder or goal you want to delete.

5. Tap the menu icon ⋮ and select **Delete**.

Tip: You can copy an event to another calendar. To do this, repeat steps 1 to 4 above and tap the menu icon ⋮ . Then tap **Copy to...** and follow the prompts.

Inviting People to Your Events

If you have an upcoming event, you can invite people to it using the Google Calendar app. To do this:

1. From the Home screen, swipe up and tap on **Calendar** .

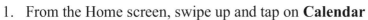

2. Tap the plus icon ⊕ at the lower right side of the screen and choose **event**.

3. To set the start and end date/time of the event, tap onscreen date/time and adjust them accordingly. If the event is an all-day event, tap the status switch next to **All-day** to activate it. When you activate all-day, you would not be able to set a specific time. To learn more about all-day event, see page 336.

4. To enter a title for your event, tap "Enter title" located at the top of the screen and enter a title. Tap **Done** on the virtual keyboard to save the title.

5. To invite people to your event, tap **Invite people** and type the name of those you are inviting. The list filters as you type. To select any suggested name, tap it. You can also enter email address if you don't have the contact of those you are inviting. Simply enter the email address and tap "Done" on the virtual keyboard. In addition, if you have a Google group, you can enter the email address of the group to send invitations to the members of the group. Tap **Done** (found at the top of the screen).

6. Fill in other details.

7. When you are done, tap **Save** (located at the top of the screen). If prompted, select **Send.**

Generally, Google will send out email invitations to the invited guests/people after you save the event. The invitees will have the opportunity to respond to the request through their emails.

Tip: To see the people coming to your event, simply open Calendar app and tap on the event.

In addition, you can send invitation to thousands of people easily if you have Google group and you have these people (you want to invite) in your Google group. To create a group, visit groups.google.com

Controlling What You See in Your Calendar

You can choose what you see in your calendar. For example, if you don't want public holidays/reminders to appear in your calendar, you can prevent it. To do this:

1. From the Home screen, swipe up and tap **Calendar** .

2. Tap the menu icon ☰ at the top of the screen.

3. Unselect those options you don't want to see in your calendar. For example, if you don't want your Reminder to populate your calendar, deselect it. Furthermore, if you don't want to see events from a Google account, you can use this method to deselect that Google account.

Managing Google Calendar App Settings

1. From the Home screen, swipe up and tap **Calendar** ![calendar icon]. Tap the menu icon ☰ at the top of the screen.

2. Scroll down and tap **Settings** (located at the bottom of the screen). Choose an option.

3. To access general settings, tap **General**. General settings allow you to manage settings like time zone, notifications, quick response etc.

4. To adjust event's notification, tap **Events.** Tap a default notification (for example, tap "30 minutes before") and choose another one. To add another notification, tap **Add another notification**. To pick another color for your event, tap **Color** and choose one.

Using the Camera

Samsung Galaxy S10, S10 Plus and S10e come with rear-facing camera(s), front-facing camera(s) and a LED flash. With these cameras, you can capture an image or record a video.

Tip: The memory capacity of the images taken might be affected by camera settings, shooting scenes and shooting conditions.

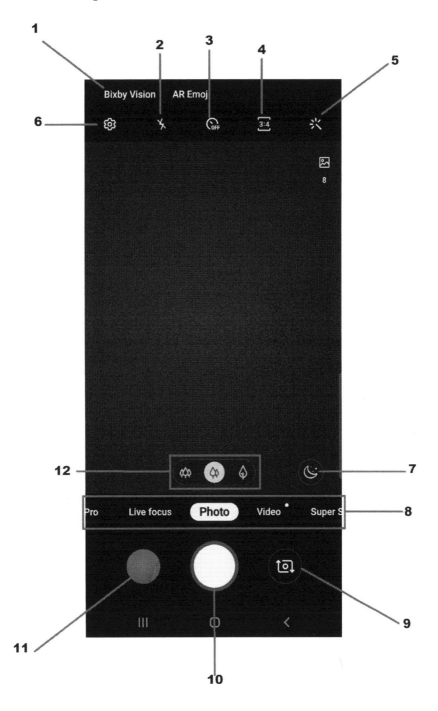

Number	Function
1.	Bixby Vision button. Tap this icon to get more information about the picture you are viewing. To learn more about Bixby vision, go to page 196.
2.	Flash light button
3.	Timer button: When you click on time button you would be able to take picture of an object after a specified time when you tap the camera button.
4.	Aspect ratio button
5.	Filters button
6.	Camera settings button
7.	Scene optimizer button
8.	Shooting mode: Camera app has many shooting modes and you would need to choose the shooting mode based on what you are doing. For example, if you are taking a picture of a waterfall, you can consider using panorama mode. To select another shooting mode, swipe left or right, or tap the name of the shooting mode.
9.	Front-facing/rear-facing camera switch
10.	Camera button
11.	Preview thumbnail
12.	Lens buttons: Choose lens based on what you want to capture, for example, if you want the picture of an object to appear closer, select .

To Capture a photo

1. While the phone is locked, double-press the Power Key (at the side of the phone) to launch the camera app. Please note that you may need to enable this feature. To do this, see the next subtopic below. Alternatively, from the app screen, tap **Camera.**

2. Aim the lens at the subject and make any necessary adjustments. To focus any part of the screen, tap that part of the screen.

3. To adjust the camera settings, tap and pick a setting.

4. Tap front-facing/rear-facing icon to switch between the front-facing and rear-facing cameras.

5. To zoom in, place two fingers on the screen and spread them apart. Do the reverse to zoom out.

6. Tap on **camera button** when you are done adjusting the settings.

Tip: You can choose to enable or disable **Quick review**. To disable/enable **Quick review**, tap the settings icon while on the camera app, scroll down and tap the switch next to **Quick review**. When the image review (Quick Review) is enabled, you will see a preview of each photo immediately after you take a picture. This allows you to immediately delete the picture if you are not satisfied with it.

Hint: To change the picture storage location to SD card, while on the camera app screen, tap the settings icon . Then scroll down and tap **Storage Location.** Select **SD card** from the option that appears.

To open the Camera by quickly pressing the Power key twice:

1. While on the camera app screen, tap the settings icon .
2. Scroll down and tap the switch next to **Quick launch** to activate it.

To customize camera settings:

1. From the app screen, tap **Camera.**

2. Tap the settings icon 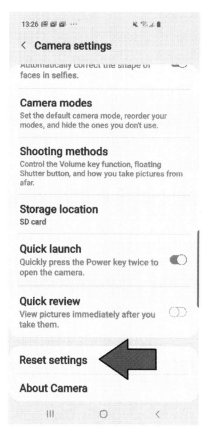.

3. Adjust the various settings as you like.

Tip: Camera settings consist of a lot of features and you may not need to adjust some of these features. In fact, the default settings are sufficient for many users.

If someone adjusts the camera settings in a way you don't like and you wish to restore the

camera settings back to factory settings, follow these steps. Tap the settings icon

while on the camera app screen, scroll down and tap **Reset settings.** Tap **Reset** when prompted.

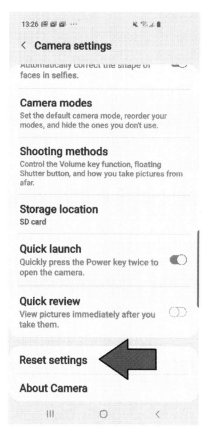

Recording a video

1. When the phone is locked, double-press the Power Key (at the side of the phone) to launch the camera app. Alternatively, from the Home screen, tap **Camera.**

2. Swipe the shooting mode tab until **Video** is selected.

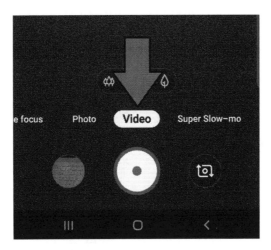

3. Tap on the video button to start recording.

4. To zoom in while recording, place two fingers on the screen and spread them apart. To zoom out, move the two fingers closer to each other.

5. When done with the recording, tap the **video button** again.

6. To view your recorded videos, go to **Gallery/Photos** app.

Editing Pictures

You can use your phone to edit pictures.

1. Swipe up the screen while on the Home screen and tap on **Gallery/Photos**.

2. Tap on the picture you want to edit.

3. Tap the **pen icon** and pick any editing tool(s).

Getting Productive With the Camera

Many people use the camera of their phone just to take pictures, but don't know that they can be using their phone camera for more productive tasks.

Interestingly, your device features a powerful camera that transforms the way you use a camera. In this section, we will be exploring ways we can be more productive with our phone camera.

Ways to be more productive with your phone camera are mentioned below:

- **Use your phone camera as a scanner for your documents**

You probably have many documents that are very important to you. Why don't you look for time to take the pictures of all these documents and save them to your phone or have them stored in the cloud. There are times that you would want to check something inside a document, but you are not at home. Saving your document on your phone should help you in a time like this. In addition, saving documents on your phone will save you time and stress because you have access to them on the go.

Top Android document scanners include **Microsoft Office Lens** and **Adobe Scan**. You can download these apps from Google Play store.

- **Take pictures of natural environment like waterfall and natural vegetation**

According to reports, looking at the pictures of natural environments like waterfalls and natural vegetations gives people pleasure and serves as coolness to one's eyes. In addition, it helps you appreciate the beautiful works of the Almighty God.

- **Declutter your life**

Do you know that you can use the camera of your phone to declutter your life? You probably have many hand-written documents, business cards, to-do list etc. lying all over the place in your home. You can take the picture of these notes so that you can remove them from your house and give them to appropriate waste recycling companies. This will create more space in your house and give you more visual ventilation.

I would advise you properly label the pictures of your hand-written documents, business cards, to-do list etc. to help you easily find them in the future. In addition, you can consider saving the pictures of your hand-written documents, business cards, to-do list etc. on *Evernote*. I suggest Evernote because it gives you the opportunity to search texts inside images.

- **Use your camera as a barcode and QR (quick response) code scanner**

Barcode and QR code are machine readable codes that are used to store information. Barcode is linear or one dimensional in nature. It basically looks like a cluster of parallel lines. On the other hand, QR code is two dimensional in nature. An example of a QR code is shown below. Interestingly, Samsung Galaxy S10, S10 Plus and S10e is capable of reading QR codes and barcodes using Bixby vision or barcode scanner apps. Many of us still take the long path of entering texts or links when we can get the same result by scanning barcode or QR code.

Example of a QR code

To use Bixby vision to scan a QR code:

1. Launch the phone camera and tap Bixby vision icon.

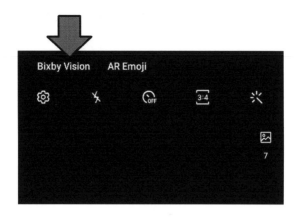

An alternate way to access Bixby Vision is tapping on Bixby Vision icon ![Bixby icon] located on the applications screen.

2. Aim your lens at the code and wait for response.

I noticed that Bixby vision can perform poorly when scanning barcodes and I would advise you install a third-party barcode scanner app. You can install a barcode scanner from Google Play store, simply search for *barcode scanner* or *QR and barcode scanner*.

- **Take the pictures of notes in meetings and lectures instead of writing them**

Taking the picture of notes after a meeting or a lecture allows you to listen during the meeting or lecture instead of writing notes.

- **Use your camera to take pictures of valuable information/documents in your life**

If you have any valuable piece of information that you can't afford to lose, use your camera to take its picture. That would serve as a backup in case of loss.

Tip: It is a good idea to back up your files/documents on cloud platforms like Dropbox, OneDrive or Google Drive.

Connectivity

Computer Connections

Your phone can be connected to a computer with a USB cable. This would enable you to transfer items such as audio, document and image files to your phone from your computer.

Warning: Do not disconnect the USB cable from a computer while the device is transferring or accessing data. This may result in data loss or damage to your phone.

Transferring content via USB

1. Connect your device to a computer with an appropriate USB cable (like the one that came with your phone).

2. When prompted to allow an access to phone data, tap **Allow.** If you don't choose Allow, your computer may not be able to access your phone.

3. Slide down from the top of the screen, tap the USB option (**USB for file transfer**) and tap it again.

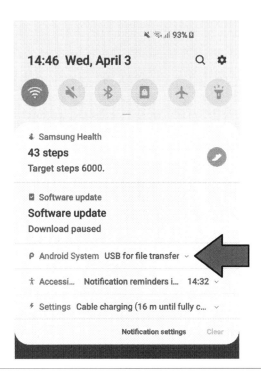

4. Tap **Transferring files** (if not selected).

5. Your device should appear in the same location where an external USB drive usually appear on your computer. For Windows users, this is typically under "This PC/Computer" menu.

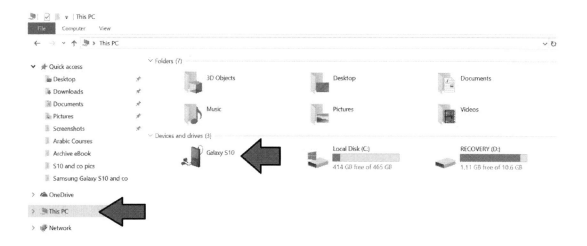

6. Open your device drive to see the different folders present. Note that you may not be able to access the folders if your phone is locked.

7. To transfer files from your computer to your phone, locate the file you want to transfer on your computer. Then click, drag and drop the file into the corresponding folder on your Phone. Alternatively, if you are using a PC, right-click on the file you want to send, select **Send to** and choose your phone from the options that appear.

8. Disconnect your phone just as you would disconnect an external memory drive. If you are using Windows 10, you may just remove the USB from the phone when you are done with the transfer. You may not need to click any disconnect icon before you remove your phone if you are using Windows 10.

Tip: After the transfer, your transferred files should appear under the corresponding content library on your device. To view any of the transferred files:

From the Home screen, swipe up and tap **Samsung folder** > **My Files**. Then tap an appropriate category to view the transferred files or folders.

In addition, you may consider installing **Files by Google** from Google Play store to manage your files better.

Note that your phone will only recognize the file you transferred if the file is a supported file type.

If you do factory reset to your phone, you may need to re-transfer the files again (unless you have them stored on a cloud storage like Dropbox).

Wi-Fi

Using your phone, you can connect to the internet or other network devices anywhere an access point or wireless hotspot is available.

To activate the Wi-Fi feature and connect to a network:

1. Swipe down from the top of the screen.

2. Tap and hold the **Wi-Fi** icon.

3. If needed, tap the switch next to Wi-Fi to turn it on.

4. Your device then automatically scans for available networks and displays them.

5. Select a network and enter a password for the network (if needed). You may also manually add a network. To manually add a network, scroll down (if necessary) and tap **Add network**. Then follow the on-screen instructions.

6. To turn Wi-Fi off, swipe down from the top of the screen and tap the Wi-Fi icon

 .

Note:

- The Wi-Fi feature running in the background will consume battery. To save battery, put it off whenever you are not using it.

- The Wi-Fi may not connect to a network if the network signal is not good.

- When Wi-Fi is connected, active and communicating with a wireless Access Point, Wi-Fi active icon is displayed on the Status bar.

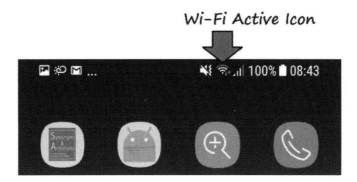

Wi-Fi Active Icon

Mobile Data

Using your phone, you can connect to the internet or other network devices using Mobile Data.

To enable mobile data:

1. Swipe down from the top of the screen.

2. Tap and hold the **Mobile data** icon  to access mobile data settings.

3. If needed, tap the switch next to **Mobile Data** to turn it on.

Please note that you may incur charges when using mobile data.

Using Your Phone as a Hotspot

If your network provider supports it, you can use this feature to share your mobile network with friends.

1. Swipe down from the top of the screen and select the settings icon . Tap **Connections** tab.

2. Tap **Mobile Hotspot and Tethering**.

3. Tap **Mobile hotspot**. If prompted to enable or disable Wi-Fi sharing, you can choose to disable Wi-Fi sharing. Wi-Fi sharing allows you to share your Wi-Fi connections with other devices, while mobile hotspot shares your mobile data with other devices. Please before you share a Wi-Fi connection with other devices, please ensures that you are not breaking any terms and conditions.

4. Turn on the switch under **Mobile Hotspot**. Please note that Wi-Fi would need to be turned off for you to turn on mobile hotspot.

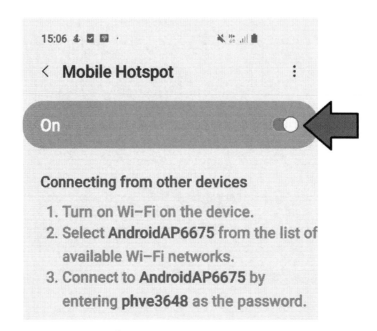

Connecting from other devices

1. Turn on Wi-Fi on the device.
2. Select **AndroidAP6675** from the list of available Wi-Fi networks.
3. Connect to **AndroidAP6675** by entering **phve3648** as the password.

5. To set the password and enable password protection, tap the menu icon ⋮ (located at the top of the screen) and tap **Configure Mobile Hotspot.** Enter a name for the network (this is the name that other devices searching for the network will see).

6. If you don't want your device (hotspot to be visible), tap **Hide my device**.

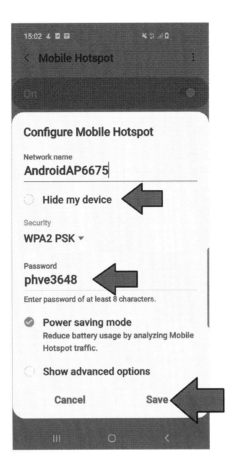

7. Scroll down and tap **Password**. Then enter a password for the network and tap **Save**.

8. After enabling the mobile hotspot, your friends should be able to connect to it just like they connect to wireless networks.

Tips:

You can choose who connects to your mobile hotspot by creating the **Allowed Device** list. To do this:

1. Follow steps 1 to 4 above.

2. Tap the menu icon ⋮ > **Allowed devices**, then tap **Add** (found at the top of the screen) to enter the device name and MAC address. The MAC address of many smart gadgets is found under **Wi-Fi settings** or **Wi-Fi Advanced settings.**

3. Tap **Add** to add the device.

4. Tap the status switch next to **Allowed devices only** to make sure only the allowed devices can connect to your mobile hotspot.

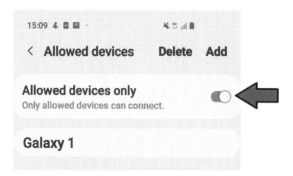

5. To delete an allowed device, tap and hold the device and select **Delete**.

In addition, you can automatically turn off Mobile hotspot if there are no connected devices. To do this, follow step 1 above. Then tap the menu icon ⋮ > **Timeout settings** and select a time.

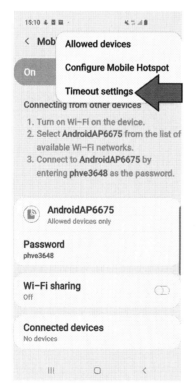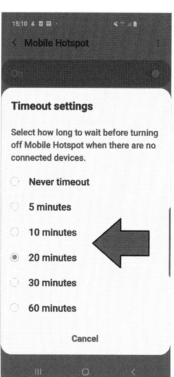

Access More by Using Bluetooth

Bluetooth option allows you to connect to another Bluetooth device within range.

Note: If there are obstacles, the operating distance of the Bluetooth may be reduced. The Bluetooth communication range is usually around 30 feet.

To use the Bluetooth feature:

1. Swipe down from the top of the screen.

2. Tap and hold the **Bluetooth** icon .
3. Then tap the status switch below the **Bluetooth**.
4. Bluetooth automatically scans for nearby Bluetooth devices and displays them. Please make sure the Bluetooth of the device you are connecting with is turned on and discoverable.
5. Tap a device to connect with and follow the prompts to finish the connection. You may need to enter a pairing code.
6. When Bluetooth is enabled, the **Bluetooth icon** would appear on the Status bar. Pairing between two Bluetooth devices should be a one-time process. Once two devices are paired, the devices may continue to recognize this connection and you may not need to re-enter a passcode.
7. To turn Bluetooth off, swipe down from the top of the screen, tap **Bluetooth** . The Bluetooth would appear gray when you turn it off (see the picture below).

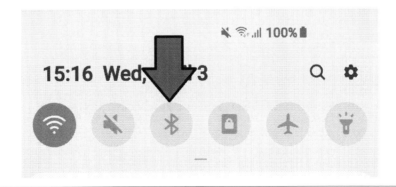

Unpairing a Paired Device

1. Swipe down from the top of the screen.

2. Tap and hold the **Bluetooth** icon.

3. Then next to **Bluetooth**, tap the status switch to turn on the Bluetooth (if not already turned on).

4. Tap the settings icon ⚙ next to the paired device and tap **Unpair** to delete the paired device.

Tip: Once you have paired your device to another device, you can rename the paired device to make it easier to recognize. To do this, follow steps 1 to 3 above and tap the settings icon ⚙ next to the previously paired device. Then tap **Rename**. Enter a new name and tap **Rename**.

Location Services

Enabling location service allows apps to serve you content related services.

To activate location services:

1. Swipe down from the top of the screen and select the settings icon ⚙. Tap **Biometrics and security**.

2. Tap **Location.**

3. Under **Location**, tap the switch to select **on.**

4. To put it off, tap the switch again.

Tip: If you want your phone to use the combination of Wi-Fi, mobile networks and sensors to estimate your location, tap **Google Location Accuracy**, then make sure it is enabled.

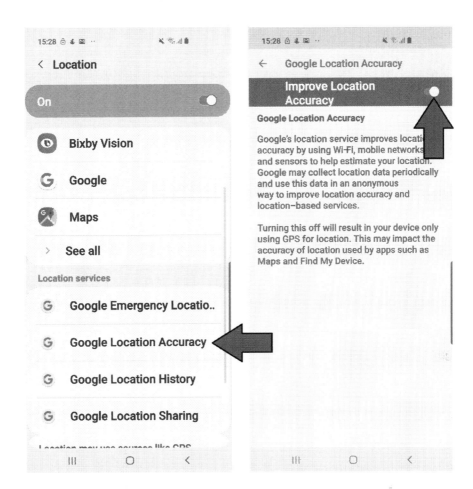

Find My Mobile

You can use this feature to locate your phone if lost.

Tip: You must sign up for a Samsung account and enable location service (as explained above) to use **Find My Mobile**.

To add Samsung account (if you have not done so before):

1. Swipe down from the top of the screen and select the settings icon .

2. Tap **Accounts and backup**.

3. Tap **Accounts**.

4. Tap **Add account**.

5. Tap **Samsung Account**. Then enter your Samsung account information.

6. Or tap **Create Account** and follow the prompts.

   Please note that if you have already added Samsung account, you can skip these steps.

To activate Find My Mobile Feature:

1. Swipe down from the top of the screen and select the settings icon .
2. Tap **Biometrics and security**.
3. Scroll down and tap **Find My Mobile**.
4. If required, enter your Samsung account password and tap **Sign In.** If you don't have a Samsung account, create one.
5. For optimal result, make sure that the status switches next to **Remote Controls**, **Google Location Service**, **Remote unlock** and **Send Last Location** are turned on.

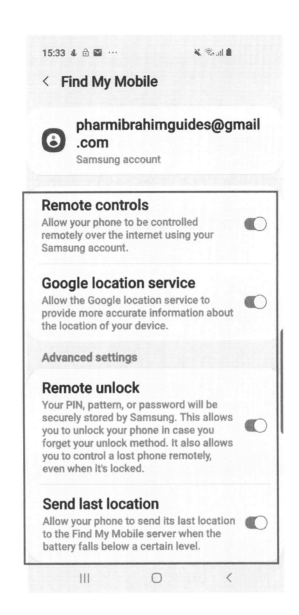

To find your lost phone:

1. Open a web browser and go to **findmymobile.samsung.com**

2. Tap **Sign In.**

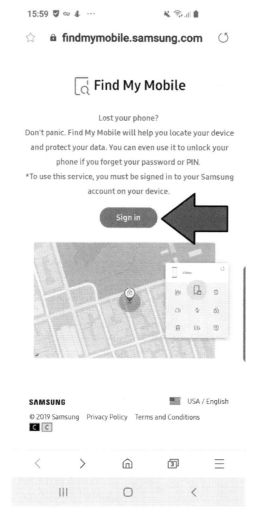

3. Enter the email address associated with your Samsung account into the email field and enter your password. Tap **Sign In.**

4. If you have more than one Samsung phone, you may need to select your Samsung Galaxy S10, S10 Plus or S10e (if it is not currently displayed). To do this, tap the menu icon ☰ next to the current device name and select your device name.

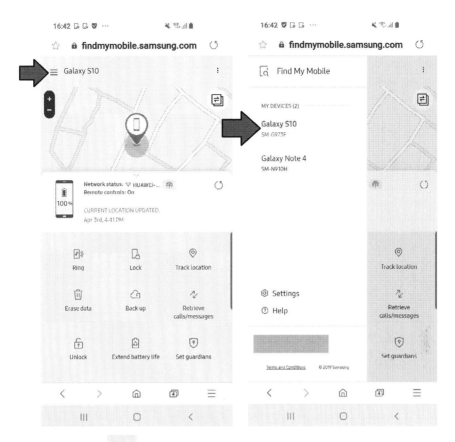

5. Tap the dropdown icon to access the map.

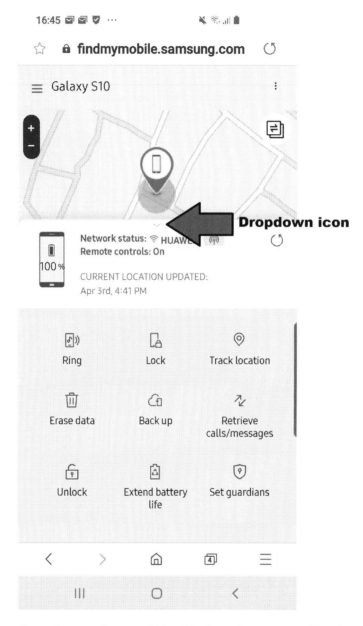

6. The current location of your phone will be displayed on a map. To close the map, tap the collapse icon ⌃.

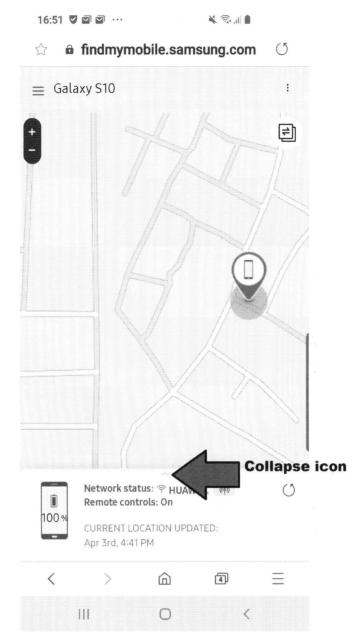

You can use the options on this website to **ring your device, lock your device, back up your device, extend battery life, set guardian, retrieve calls/messages, and wipe/erase your device**.

Tip: You can use **Find My Device** to unlock your device when you forget your log in information. To do this, follow steps 1-4 above and tap **Unlock**. Then enter your Samsung account password (if needed).

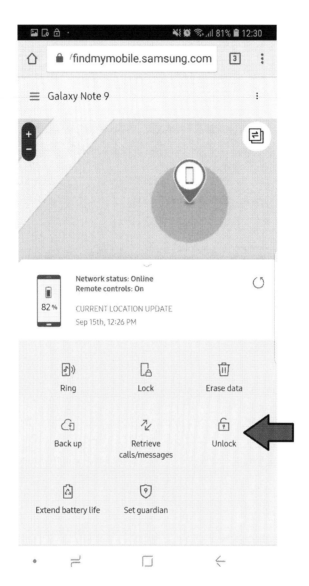

Note: Please note that your phone may need to be connected to a wireless or mobile network to be able to use the **Find My Mobile** feature to manage your phone. However, by following the method above, you may still be able to know the last known location of your phone even if not connected.

Using the NFC (Near Field Communication)

This is a technology like Bluetooth and Wi-Fi. It utilizes electromagnetic radio frequency. Devices using NFC may be passive or active. A passive device is not powered by a battery but contains information that other devices can read but does not read any information itself. An example of a passive NFC is NFC tag. On the other hand, an active NFC device can read information and send it. An example of an active NFC device is your Samsung Galaxy device.

You can use NFC feature to send files from your phone to other NFC supported devices.

To turn on and use NFC:

1. Swipe down from the top of the screen using two fingers, then tap and hold the

   NFC icon ![NFC icon] for two seconds. Please note that you may need to swipe to the right to access more quick settings icons before you can see the **NFC** icon.

2. Under **NFC and payment,** tap the switch to turn it on. Also make sure the status switch next to **Android Beam** is turned on.

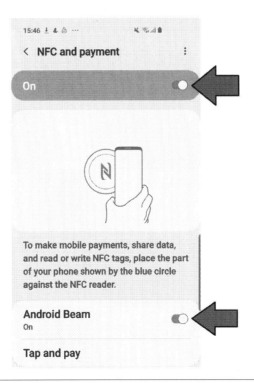

3. To use NFC to send a file to another device, ensure both devices involved have their NFC turned on. Then open the file you wish to send. Hold your mobile phone and the receiving device back to back. When **Touch to beam** appears on the screen, tap the screen to send the file.

It may not be very effective in sending large files because it may be slow.

Using NFC to make payments

In recent times, NFC is finding more usage in payment system.

Making payments with NFC:

1. Follow steps 1 and 2 above (under **To turn on and use NFC**).
2. Touch the back of your device to the NFC card reader.

Usually, after you have enabled NFC payments on your phone, and you have register for mobile payment service, you should be able to make payments for items by tapping your phone against a participating store's NFC reader.

To register for mobile payment service, please contact your payment service provider.

You can select the default payment application you want to use for making purchases on your device if you have more than one payment method installed. To do this, when on **NFC and payment** screen, tap **Tap and pay** and tap **PAYMENT** (located at the bottom of the screen). Then select a default payment app.

Settings

Settings menu give you the opportunity to customize your device as you like.

To access the settings menu

1. Swipe down from the top of the screen and select the settings icon .
2. Alternatively, swipe up from the Home screen and tap **Settings**.
3. Tap a setting category.

Search for Settings

It is advisable to use the searching feature when you are not sure exactly where to find a certain setting.

1. Swipe down from the top of the screen and select the settings icon 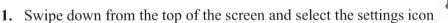 .
2. Tap search icon 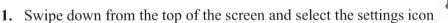 found at the top of the screen.
3. Enter a word or words in the Search field. The list filters as you write.
4. Tap an option (make sure you select the best match).

Tip: There is a tip to getting what you want from your device. From time to time, you would want to customize your phone in a special way. All you need to do to get started is

to open the settings as described above. Then tap the search icon 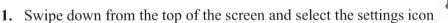 and enter a search word or phrase corresponding to what you want to do.

What You Must Know About Samsung Galaxy S10, S10 Plus or S10e

How to Find Your Phone When lost

As a human being, it is not impossible that you misplace your phone. If someone else (a thief) has not taken custody of it, there are steps to follow to find it. These steps have been discussed at length on page 361 to 368; please refer to it for details.

Staying Productive While Using Your Samsung Galaxy S10, S10 Plus or S10e

Smartphones are cool things to have, but if you are not careful, they might get you entangled. Many people spend less time with friends and family because of their phone. They enjoy pressing their phones all the time even if it adds little or no meaning to their lives.

The truth is that if you want to stay productive, you must know when to drop your phone and do things that are more important to you. You must know when to switch off your phone or avoid using the internet. I have noticed that it is easier said than done. For most of us, it is difficult to drop our phones (and avoid online chats) to attend to other important things. What I have personally observed is that many of us need an outside help. One of the beautiful things we need is a good software (application) to make us accountable and prevent internet/app access when we are tempted.

Cold Turkey app is one of the apps out there that can help you block apps on your phone (for a specified time) so that you can concentrate on other things. You can download **Cold Turkey** app on Google Play store.

In addition, if you are looking for an accountable app that will enable you to know how you spend your time, you can try RescueTime Time Management app. This app will let you know how you spend your time on your phone. It will also let you know how productive you are. You can learn more and download **RescueTime Time Management** app from Google Play store.

Finally, another application that you could use to avoid distractions and block apps is Freedom app. You can download Freedom app from Google Play store. Simply search for **Freedom Block Distractions**.

How to Reduce Data Usage on Samsung Galaxy S10, S10 Plus or S10e

If you realize that you use more data than normal, there are steps to follow to reduce your data consumption.

1. The first thing is to make sure that you update apps on Wi-Fi only. To do this:
   a. Swipe up from the Home screen and tap **Play Store**.
   b. Swipe in from the left edge of the screen.
   c. Tap **Settings**.
   d. Tap **Auto-update apps** and select **Over Wi-Fi only** or **Don't auto-update apps.** Then select **Done.**
2. Consider using a data friendly browser.

3. Enable Data saver: To do this, from a Home screen, tap the settings icon . Tap **Connections**. Tap **Data usage** and tap **Data saver**. Tap the status switch under **Data saver**.

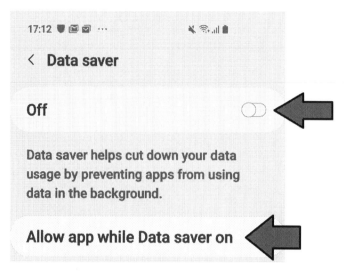

To control the number of apps that have unrestricted access to your data, tap **Allow app while Data saver on** (see the picture above).

4. Use **Datally** app. This app allows you to save and control the use of your data. To download Datally, visit Google Play store.

Solution to Non-Responding Apps

Sometimes, an app may start misbehaving and may even refuse to close. The first thing you can do in a situation like this is to tap on the recent button ▐▐▐ . This gives you access to all opened/running apps on your phone. Locate this app and swipe it up to close it. Try launching the app again.

If it keeps misbehaving after closing it or it refuses to close, then you may try these steps:

1. Swipe down from the top of the screen and select the settings icon .
2. Tap **Apps**.
3. Then tap on the misbehaving application from the list of applications.
4. Select **FORCE STOP**. This will stop the app from carrying out any process on your phone. To enable the app again, just launch the app.

5. If you want to clear all your data on the app and start using it like a new app, tap **Storage** and select **Clear data**.

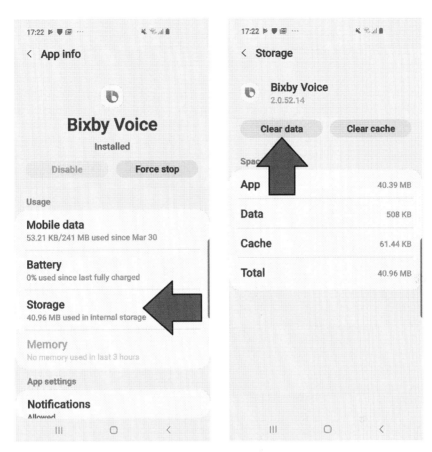

Tip: Please restart your device if stopping an app causes your device to stop working correctly. *In addition, force stopping an app may cause error(s).*

How to Conserve Your Galaxy Device's Battery Life

You may discover that you have to charge your Galaxy device twice in 24 hours to keep it running. There are steps to follow to ensure that your phone serves you throughout the day with just a single charge.

1. **Reduce the screen brightness and turn off the automatic brightness:** I have realized over time that high screen brightness level consumes a lot of energy. There is usually a substantial difference between using a phone with a maximum

brightness level and using it with a moderate brightness level. As a rule, don't use your phone with a maximum brightness level unless you can't see what is on the screen clearly. For example, if you are outdoor. Make sure you reduce it immediately when it is no more needed.

To reduce the screen brightness, swipe down from the top of the screen using two fingers. Then use the small circle on the slider to adjust the brightness level.

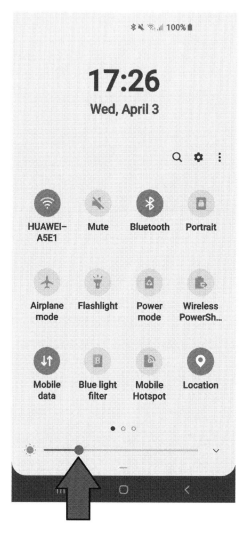

In addition, to enable adaptive brightness (so that your phone adjusts its brightness based on your usage/lighting conditions), tap the dropdown arrow ∨. Then tap the switch next to **Adaptive brightness**.

2. **Shorten the Screen timeout:** If you really want to save your battery life, you must try to shorten the screen timeout. Reducing how long your phone would stay lit up after you finish interacting with it will help you save your battery. To manage the screen timeout setting:

   a. Swipe down from the top of the screen and select the settings icon .

   b. Tap **Display**.

   c. Scroll down and tap on **Screen Timeout**. Then choose an option.

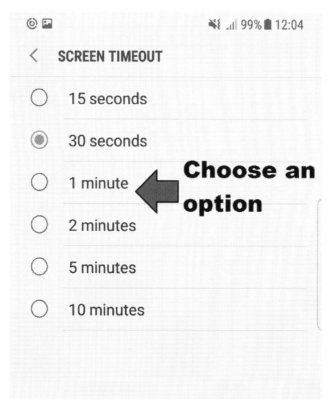

3. **Turn off Wi-Fi, Mobile Hotspot and Bluetooth:** When you are not using Wi-Fi. Mobile hotspot or Bluetooth, please always remember to put them off. These features really consume energy and they are better off when not in use.

4. **Reduce number of notifications:** There are two benefits of doing this. The first is that there will be less distractions and the second benefit is that it conserves energy. Limit yourself to those notifications that are important to you. To manage notification setting for an app:

   a. Swipe down from the top of the screen and select the settings icon .

   b. Tap **Apps**.

   c. Tap an app.

   d. Tap on **Notifications** to configure the notifications setting for the chosen app. To disable the notification for an app, tap the indicator switch next to **Show notifications**.

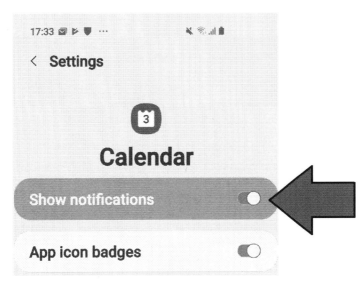

5. **Close all unnecessary apps:** The truth is that any app you access consumes part of the limited battery energy. It is important to close any app you are not using from time to time. To access all apps currently running on your phone, tap on the recent button ▐▐▐, then swipe up the application you want to close. You can also put apps to sleep. To learn how to do this, please go to page 19.

6. **Use the correct charger:** Using a wrong charger can endanger the health of your phone/battery and it is better to avoid such practices.

7. **Consider switching off your phone:** If you are not going to use your phone for an extended period, you may consider switching it off.

What to Do if You Forget Your Device Lock Screen Password/Pin

1. Open a web browser and go to **findmymobile.samsung.com**

2. Tap **Sign In**.

3. Enter the email address associated with your Samsung account into the email field and enter your password. Tap **Sign In.**

4. If you have more than one Samsung phone, you may need to select your Samsung Galaxy S10, S10 Plus or S10e (if it is not currently displayed). To do this, tap the menu icon ☰ next to the current device name and select your device name.

5. Tap **Unlock** and enter your Samsung account password.

Note: Your phone may need to be connected to a wireless or mobile network to be able to use the **Find My Mobile** feature to unlock your phone.

In addition, please note that if you have disabled **Remote Controls/Remote unlock**, you would need to activate it before you can use the method above. To do this:

1. Swipe down from the top of the screen and select the settings icon .
2. Tap **Biometrics and security**.
3. Tap **Find My Mobile**.

4. If needed, enter your Samsung account information and tap **Sign In**. If you don't have a Samsung account, create one.

5. Make sure that the status switches next to **Remote Controls**, and **Remote unlock** are turned on.

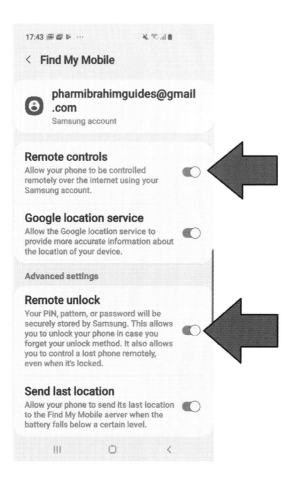

How to Take Screenshots on Your Device

Another task you can perform on your device is taking a screenshot.

To take a screenshot with your device, please follow the instructions below:

Method 1

Press and hold the volume down key and the power key simultaneously for one second.

You can view captured images in Gallery.

Method 2

You can also capture screenshots by swiping your hand to the left or right across the screen. To be able to use this method, you have to enable it first. To do this:

1. Swipe down from the top of the screen and select the settings icon .
2. Scroll down and tap **Advanced features** and then select **Motions and gestures**.
3. Tap **Palm swipe to capture** and tap the status switch to activate it.

To capture a screenshot when this feature is enabled, just swipe the edge of your hand across more than half of the screen. Please note that this method will not work while the keyboard is shown.

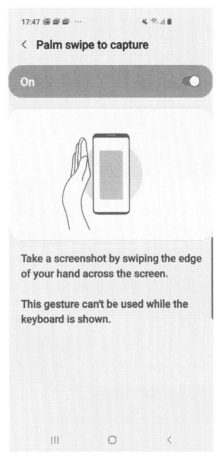

The Smart Capture

You can capture a screen and the scrollable area. In addition, you can immediately crop and share the captured screen. This feature is usually enabled by default, but if you want to check whether it is enabled or not, please follow the instructions below:

1. Swipe down from the top of the screen and select the settings icon .
2. Scroll down and tap **Advanced features**.
3. Tap **Smart capture** and tap the status switch to activate it.

Thereafter, press and hold the volume down key and the power key simultaneously to take a screenshot. Then tap on any of the options below:

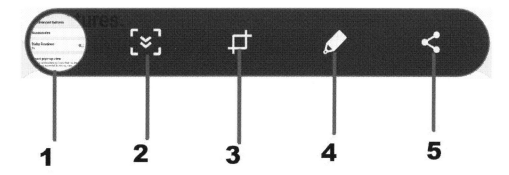

1. **Image Preview**: Tap this icon to view the screenshot.
2. **Scroll Capture**: Use this to capture the hidden parts of the screen. When you tap this icon, the screen would automatically scroll down and more contents would be captured. To capture more screens, tap this icon again.
3. **Crop:** Use this to crop a portion from the screenshot.
4. **Draw:** Use this option to annotate the screenshot.
5. **Share**: Use this to share the screenshot.

Extras

What You Must Know Before Selling or Giving Away Your Samsung Galaxy S10, S10 Plus or S10e

A time would probably come when you may need to give away or sell your Samsung Galaxy S10, S10 Plus or S10e. There are few things you must know before this time comes.

Some time ago, BBC reported that Avast (an antivirus giant) was able to use publicly available forensic security tools to extract naked selfies from second-hand phones bought on eBay. Other extracted data were emails, text messages and Google searches.

It is usual for many users to perform factory resets before selling their phones. The truth is that with the advent of more sophisticated software, factory reset is no more enough. In fact, you have to go a step further.

So, what can you do to save your privacy? The simple answer is to go a step further by always encrypting your files. You should encrypt all your data before performing factory reset when you are considering selling or giving away your Phone.

However, you must know that encrypting your device before doing the factory reset may not give 100% protection to your privacy. Who knows if programmers will develop a software that would be a step ahead of that in the nearest future? The best way to completely protect your privacy is to destroy your phone when you don't need it again. But as you know, this is not feasible all the time and may not be advisable.

Finally, encrypting your phone before performing factory reset is an efficient way of protecting your privacy. At least it makes it much more difficult for people to retrieve your files.

Interestingly, Samsung Galaxy S10, S10 Plus or S10e automatically encrypts data stored on it. However, you would need to encrypt data stored on memory card yourself. To do that:

- From the Home screen, swipe up from the bottom of the screen and tap **Settings**.

- Tap **Biometrics and security** > **Encrypt SD card**.

- Read the onscreen information and if you are satisfied with it, tap **Encrypt SD card**.

When you encrypt your memory card, you may need a numeric PIN or password to decrypt your SD card when you first access it after switching on your device.

Tip: You would need to reset your phone to factory settings before selling or giving it away. This would ensure you delete all your data on it. If necessary, make sure you back up your files before performing factory reset.

To remove all the data on your phone:

1. Swipe down from the top of the screen and select the settings icon .
2. Scroll down and tap **General management**.
3. Tap **Reset**.
4. Tap **Factory data reset**.
5. Scroll down (if needed) and tap **Reset**.

Travelling with Your Phone—What to Know

While travelling abroad with your Samsung Galaxy S10, S10 Plus or S10e, there are a few things to know. These things are discussed below.

1. Unlock your phone and plan to get a local SIM card

If you are travelling abroad, it is important you consider unlocking your phone to use foreign SIM cards on your phone. Generally, you can unlock your phone by contacting your network service provider. If your phone is already unlocked, then have a clear plan to get a local SIM card when you get to the foreign land. Generally, using a local SIM card for your calls will save your money than roaming.

Note: If you are unable to unlock your phone and you want to stay several months abroad, consider buying a cheap unlocked phone.

2. Get to know about roaming

If you are not planning to unlock your phone or get a local SIM card, then I would recommend that you know about the roaming plans of your network service provider. You can easily do this by contacting your network service provider.

3. Set up a lock screen

It is important to set up a lock screen while going abroad. This would save you a lot of stress if you misplace the phone. Security in some places in the world is bad and your phone can easily be snatched from you.

Even if your phone is not stolen, you can misplace your phone while moving from one place to another. If you have set up a screen lock, you can be sure that it would be extremely hard (if not impossible) for people to access your data from the lost phone. To know how to set up a lock screen, go to page 139. I would advise you to use a lock screen password (if you can) for your device. A lock screen password appears more secured than pattern or PIN.

Tip: If you mistakenly misplace your phone, you may locate it by following the instructions on page 361-368.

4. Get a power bank (USB Battery Pack)

Charging your phone might not be easy while abroad. I would advise you consider getting a power bank to charge your phone. You can get a cheap and reliable power bank from Amazon.

5. Monitor and save your data

Data are quite expensive in some countries of the world. I would advise you monitor and save data as much as you can. To know how to save data on your phone, see page 373.

6. Be careful when using Wireless network

Using a wireless network in a foreign country demands extra care. There are some countries that are notorious for hacking. I would recommend you research about any country you are visiting to know how best to prepare. To learn how to stay secured when connected to wireless, see page 392.

7. Get familiar with Google Translate

If the country you are visiting does not speak your language, then you need someone or something to help you with language translation. Interestingly, Google Translate might provide some help in this regard. To start using Google Translate, visit **https://translate.google.com**

8. Get familiar with the Google Map application

Google Map is one of the best map applications in the world. You can easily know the route to your destination using this app. I would advise you familiarize yourself with Google Map before traveling. This application can save you a lot of stress and time. You can download **Google Map** from Google Play store.

Getting an Antivirus for Your Phone -- Is It Necessary?

Many people may not really take the issue of antivirus seriously because they think that virus software target PCs much more than phones. The truth is that the world is changing and the best thing you can do is to always be on guard.

Interestingly, there is a device protection on Samsung Galaxy S10, S10 Plus and S10e, to access this protection:

- From the Home screen, swipe up from the bottom of the screen and tap **Settings**.

- Tap **Device care**

- Tap **Security** (located at the lower right part of the screen).

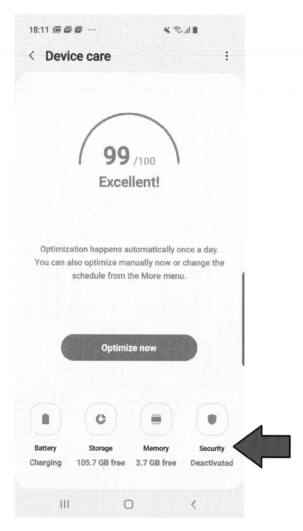

- Read the terms and conditions and select **Agree/Activate** to continue.
- To scan your phone, tap on **Scan Phone**.

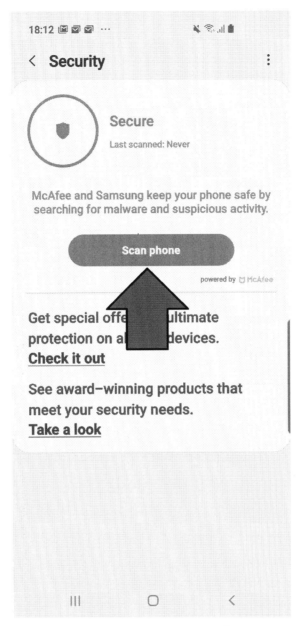

Please note that you may not have this antivirus option if your network service provider or region does not support it.

In addition, there are many reputable free antiviruses on Google Play store. My favorite antiviruses are AVG, Lookout and Norton Antiviruses. You may check Google Play Store to download any of these.

Note: The best way to protect yourself from a virus attack is being proactive. For example, I don't expect you to click links from unsolicited emails. So, having many antiviruses on your phone may not help if you are not prudent in your actions.

Safety Precautions When Using Samsung Galaxy S10, S10 Plus and S10e on Wi-Fi

With many free Wi-Fi hotspots around, it is likely that you are going to find yourself using Wi-Fi more on your phone. There are a few things to keep in mind when using Wi-Fi.

1. Confirm the Network Name

Hackers sometimes set up a fake Wi-Fi network in order to tap into the information of unwitting public users. To avoid this, make sure you are sure of the name of the network you are connecting to. You may ask any trusted individual around you if you doubt the name of a network.

2. Connect to a Secure Site

Whenever you are sending a sensitive information, always make sure that the site is a secured website. You can know whether a website is a secure site or not by checking whether the *url* address of the website starts with **HTTPS.** If it starts with https, then it should be a secured site. However, please note that some websites might start with https but are still unsecured. Anyway, browsing apps like Google Chrome would usually warn you when visiting websites like these.

3. Run an Antivirus Software

As earlier mentioned, using an antivirus is very crucial in today's world. You may consider installing a genuine antivirus. There are many of them on Google Play store.

4. Get a Virtual Private Network (VPN)

It is highly important you use a virtual private network when using a public wireless network. There are both free and paid VPN providers. My favorite is **Hotspot Shield VPN.** It is available on Google Play store.

They offer both free and paid versions. You may also check out other VPN apps to pick the best.

5. Avoid Automatic Connection

Make sure your Wi-Fi is off when not using it to avoid your phone automatically connecting to an open network. Turning your Wi-Fi off when not using it will also save your battery.

My Love for My Samsung Galaxy Device Is Reducing; What Should I Do?

It is possible that after buying Samsung Galaxy S10, S10 Plus or S10e, you realize that it performs below your expectation. It is likely that you dislike your phone because of a software or hardware issue. Generally, the hardware has to do with the design, the phone make up, the weight of the phone etc. While the software has to do with the OS and applications.

If your love for your Samsung Galaxy device is reducing because of the software, there is a way out. You can take your time to look for beneficial apps to install on your device.

If your love for your Samsung Galaxy device is reducing because of the hardware, then you could consider learning how to live with it (you may have to force yourself to love it), giving it away or selling it. If you are considering selling your phone or giving it away, then make sure you read the article on page 385-387.

TROUBLESHOOTING

If the touch screen responds slowly or improperly or your phone is not responding, try the following:

- Remove any protective covers (screen protector) from the touch screen.
- Ensure that your hands are clean and dry when tapping. In addition, ensure that the screen of your phone is not wet. If wet, use a soft dry towel to clean it.
- Press the power button once to lock the screen and press it again to unlock the screen and enter a PIN/password/pattern if required.
- Restart your device.

Your phone doesn't charge

- Make sure you are using an appropriate Samsung charger to charge your phone.
- If your Samsung Galaxy device does not indicate that it is charging, unplug the power adapter and restart your device.
- Make sure you use the USB cable that came with your Samsung Galaxy device or any that has similar specs.

Your device is hot to the touch

When you use applications that require more power or use applications on your device for an extended period, your phone may be a bit hot. This is normal and it should not have much effect on its performance. You may just allow your phone to rest for some time or close some applications.

Your phone freezes or has fatal error

If your phone freezes or it is unresponsive, press and hold the Power key and the Volume Down key simultaneously until the screen goes off, then wait for it to restart automatically. Please note that you may need to press the Power key and the Volume Down key simultaneously for more than 5 seconds before the phone will restart.

Phone does not connect to Wi-Fi

Make sure you don't have limited network connectivity in that area. If your network signal is good and you still cannot connect, you may perform any of these actions.

- Make sure your Airplane Mode is off.
- Try restarting the Wi-Fi.
- Move closer to your router and scan for the available networks. If the network still does not show up, you may add the network manually.
- Restart your router and modem. Unplug the modem and router for a few minutes and plug the modem in, then the router.
- Try restarting your phone.

Phone screen color is appearing somehow

- Check if you have not mistakenly turned on blue light filter. To do this, go to

  Settings  **> Display > Blue Light Filter > Turn on now**.

Another Bluetooth device is not located

- Ensure Bluetooth feature is activated on your phone and the device you want to connect to.
- Ensure that your phone and the other Bluetooth device are within the maximum Bluetooth range (usually around 30 feet).

A connection is not established when you connect your phone to a PC using USB cable

- Ensure that the USB cable you are using is compatible with your device and can transfer files.
- Ensure the USB port on your computer/phone is working properly.
- Ensure that you have the proper drivers installed and updated on your PC.

Audio quality is poor during a call

- Ensure that the network signal is strong. When you are in an area with a weak or poor reception, you may lose reception. Try moving to another area and try again.

Safety Precautions

A. To prevent electric shock, fire and explosion

1. Do not use damaged power cords or plugs or loose electrical sockets.
2. Do not touch the power cord with a wet hand.
3. Do not bend or damage the power cord.
4. Do not short-circuit the charger.
5. Do not use your phone during thunderstorm.
6. Do not dispose your phone by putting it in fire.

B. Follow all safety warnings and regulations when using your device in restricted areas.

C. Comply with all safety warnings and regulations regarding mobile device usage while operating a vehicle.

D. Proper care and use of your phone

1. Do not use or store your phone in a very hot or cold area.
2. Do not put your phone near magnetic fields.
3. Do not use camera flash close to eyes of people or pets because it can cause temporary loss of vision or damage the eyes.
4. When speaking on the phone, speak directly into the mouthpiece.
5. Avoid disturbing others when using your phone in public.
6. Keep your phone away from children because they may mistakenly damage it as it may seem like a toy to them.

Just Before You Go (Please Read!)

Although I have put in tremendous effort in writing this guide,

I am confident that I have not said it all.

I have no doubt believing that I have not written everything possible about Samsung Galaxy S10, S10 Plus and S10e.

So, I want you to do me a favor.

If you would like to know how to perform a task that is not included in this guide, please let me know by sending me an email at **pharmibrahimguides@gmail.com**. I will try as much as possible to reply you as soon as I can.

You may also visit my author's page at **www.amazon.com/author/pharmibrahim**

And please don't forget to follow me when you visit my author's page. Simply click or tap on the **Follow** button located below the profile picture.

Index

Unlock phone

Made in the
USA
Monee, IL